Landscape Liturgies

Landscape Liturgies

Resources to celebrate and bless the earth

Nick Mayhew-Smith
with
Sarah Brush

CANTERBURY
PRESS
Norwich

© Nick Mayhew-Smith and Sarah Brush 2021

First published in 2021 by the Canterbury Press Norwich
Editorial office
3rd Floor, Invicta House
108–114 Golden Lane
London EC1Y 0TG, UK
www.canterburypress.co.uk

Canterbury Press is an imprint of Hymns Ancient & Modern Ltd
(a registered charity)

Hymns Ancient & Modern® is a registered trademark of
Hymns Ancient & Modern Ltd
13A Hellesdon Park Road, Norwich,
Norfolk NR6 5DR, UK

Scripture quotations are from New Revised Standard Version Bible: Anglicized
Edition, copyright © 1989, 1995 National Council of the Churches of Christ in the
United States of America. Used by permission. All rights reserved worldwide.

British Library Cataloguing in Publication data

A catalogue record for this book is available
from the British Library

978 1-78622-380 7

Typeset by Regent Typesetting
Printed and bound in Great Britain by
CPI Group (UK) Ltd

CONTENTS

Acknowledgements   xi

Foreword   xiii

Introduction   xv

1 ANIMAL BLESSINGS   1

Blessing of the Bees and Hives   3

The Prayer of St Mammes for Animals   7

Blessing of the Animals on St Francis Day   9

St Bride's Charm for Animal Blessings   17

Liturgies of Animal Care   18

    1 Celebrating the Creatures   19

    2 A Service for Animal Welfare   24

Blessing of the Animals: A Short Service   31

The Prayer of St Modestus for Animals   33

Blessing for Animal Welfare Staff and Sanctuaries   35

Prayer at the Death of Companion Animals   37

2 LOVE FEASTS AND COMMUNITY GATHERINGS   39

Liturgy for a Love-Feast: A Time of Centring   42

Liturgy for a Love-Feast: Katrina's Dream   45

Liturgy for a Love-Feast: UK Methodist Version   47

3 CHURCHYARD, PARISH AND ROGATION
  BLESSING RITUALS   50

  Clipping Service   53

  Two Blessings of Green Things: Crops, Grass and Herbs   57

  The Blessing of Public Utilities: Roman Catholic Order   59

  A Traditional Rogation Liturgy   63

  An Elizabethan Rogation Day Service   70

  Blessing of a Bridge, Road and Other Means of
  Transport: Roman Catholic Order   79

  Prayers for Street Pastors   83

  Blessing of a Sports Field or Gymnasium:
  Roman Catholic Order   86

  Visiting a Cemetery: Roman Catholic Order   90

4 WATER BLESSINGS AND RITUALS   95

  Well Blessing from the *Bobbio Missal*   97

  Three Anglo-Saxon Water Prayers   98

  The Great Blessing of the Waters   101

  Blessing of the River from a Bridge   114

  Blessing of the Waters: The Syrian Ritual   119

  Sea Sunday Service and Blessing of Boats   128

    1 Sea Sunday Service and Blessing of Boats   129

    2 Choral Evensong for Sea Sunday   132

  Sea and Ocean Blessings from the *Carmina Gadelica* 140

    1 The Ocean Blessing   141

    2 Ocean Blessing   142

    3 Sea Prayer   143

  Blessing of Boats and Fishing Gear: Roman Catholic
  Short Rite   144

5 TREE BLESSINGS AND GATHERINGS   145

A Tree-planting Liturgy   147

A Tree-planting Eucharist   151

A Toast to a Tree   158

A Prayer Over Trees and Vines   159

   1 A Prayer Over Vines   159

   2 A Prayer Over Fruit-Bearing Trees   159

An Early Medieval Tree Blessing   160

6 FIELDS, HILLS, WEATHER AND AGRICULTURE   161

A Service for the Apparition of St Michael the Archangel   164

Field Blessings from Anglo-Saxon England   169

The Prayer of St Tryphon for the Protection of Gardens, Fields and Crops   172

Blessing of Seeds at Planting Time: Short Order Roman Catholic Rite   174

The Æcerbot Field Blessing Ritual   175

Blessing of First Grain and Blessing of a Bakery   179

   1 The Blessing of the Grain for the First Milling   179

   2 Blessing of a Bakery   180

A Reaping Blessing from the *Carmina Gadelica*   181

Two Blessings: For Apples and First Fruits in Anglo-Saxon Tradition   183

   1 Blessing of Apples   183

   2 Blessing of New Fruits   183

Harvest Blessing from the Apostolic Tradition   184

Blessing of Grapes and Beans   185

A Prayer Against Lightning   186

Order for the Blessing of Fields and Flocks: Roman Catholic Order   187

7 PILGRIMAGE PRAYERS AND BLESSINGS 191

Anglo-Saxon Journey Blessings 192

   1 For Those Going on a Journey 192

   2 For Those Going on a Journey 193

An Irish Blessing For Travellers 194

Prayer for Travelling 195

Prayer to St James Prayed While Walking the *Camino* 196

The Blessing of Pilgrims: Roman Catholic Order 197

A Prayer Over Pilgrims from the *Sarum Missal* 201

A Service for Pilgrims and Travellers 209

Anglo-Saxon or Celtic Journey Charm 213

Prayer for One who Intends to Go on a Journey 215

Bibliography 216

Acknowledgement of Sources 219

Further Reading and Resources 221

Notes 223

List of Illustrations 227

Dedicated to Richard and Christine Mayhew-Smith,
parents of the author and lovers of a good landscape

ACKNOWLEDGEMENTS

This book is a compilation and hence a collaboration with so many leaders, thinkers and pioneers from churches both ancient and modern. So many have made a personal contribution to the principal author Nick Mayhew-Smith, and to this project, offering support, advice and in many cases supplying the liturgies and rituals themselves. The idea for this book arose during a conversation with Dr Tim Macquiban and Dr Clive Norris at the Southlands Methodist Trust, University of Roehampton, discussing ways in which the church can offer a positive and creative response to the problems of environmental degradation and global heating. The overall project and this book have been shaped by Sue Miller, director of the Susanna Wesley Foundation, and Dr Christopher Stephens, head of Southlands College, both at the University of Roehampton, and greatly supported by Professor Tina Beattie. Its reference group of project supporters includes Bishop Richard Cheetham, Dr Ruth Valerio, Revd Augusto Zampini, Revd Ermal Kirby, Revd Dr Martin Poulsom and Dr Ashley Cocksworth. Others who have offered advice and ideas are Professor John Eade, Dr Clare Watkins, Dr Sanjee Perera, Fr Stephen Platt, Dr Helen Gittos, Revd Mark Earey, Mark Rowland, Revd Ian Tattum, Dr Nathan Ristuccia, Dr Henry Parkes, Dr Emma Pavey, Dr Lia Shimada, Professor Dana Robert, Dr Julian Gotobed, Dr Ralph Lee and Revd Dr John Binns. Particular thanks are due to those who have contributed actual liturgical material, credited accordingly within the book itself, or helped to source it for this volume: Professor Karen Jolly, Helene de Boissiere-Swanson, Dr Cynthia Wilson, Professor Andrew Linzey, Jill Cawley, Professor Inus Daneel, Revd Jane Held, Geoffrey Kiddy, Revd Nick Utphall, Revd Barbara Allen, Revd Gary Kriss, Dr Christina Nellist, Fr Simon Peter Nellist, Bishop Michael Ipgrave and Revd Andrew Nunn. And on a personal note much thanks go to Anna and Sasha, keeping alive the Orthodox angle of this book in our home and in our own adventures into the landscape.

FOREWORD

The Susanna Wesley Foundation (SWF) is delighted to have sponsored the research and writing of *Landscape Liturgies*. We hope it will provide an impetus for churches, and those who have usually gathered inside them, to step outside and renew their spiritual connection with the natural world, joining with others who want to honour and celebrate the places and outdoor spaces around them.

SWF is part of Southlands Methodist Trust, based at the University of Roehampton. The Foundation funds research, encourages dialogue, and produces practical resources for churches and those who work in them. Its ultimate purpose is to contribute to the flourishing of communities. This book is part of that endeavour and part of a project that is focused on finding positive ways for us all to interact with our environment. Our approach is a positive one, underpinned by a theological discourse for releasing energy and enthusiasm into our common ecosystem to enable flourishing for all.

INTRODUCTION

When Christians move their worship outdoors, interesting things start to happen. This book was inspired by a conversation about the earliest years of the Methodists, the reform movement that took to the parks, streets and open spaces of Britain in the eighteenth century with bracing effect. Its messages of reform and renewal blew like a stiff breeze through the institutions of the established church, sweeping up many with its enthusiasm for fresh thinking and wider horizons. A survey of church history soon reveals that Methodism is just one of many expressions of Christian faith which has found cause to conduct a variety of meetings, services, liturgies and prayers in the open air.

Many and varied are the reasons behind such an impulse to take Christian worship beyond the four walls of the church, but all of them bear witness to the widest possible potential for ritual and liturgy to flourish in the great outdoors. Some, such as the Methodists, were improvising after finding the church doors closed to them. Others have found that outdoor ritual patterns work well as a way of connecting communities to the places where they live, holding services at important points in the landscape. And still others have been spurred on by a wish to extend the church's ritual action to encompass all of creation, out of a sympathy for the natural world.

From the earliest church right up to the modern day there are numerous rituals, blessings, liturgies and worship events that can take place beyond the confines of the church building. The most visible expressions in the British landscape today are Remembrance Sunday services at war memorials, Palm Sunday and Good Friday processions, and in recent decades a revival of Rogationtide and its route around the parish. Resources in this book will enable churches and related faith organizations such as schools to continue that trajectory outwards, to make further meaningful connections and positive interactions with the wider world. People flourish as surely as any flower or tree when they find a place to put down roots, make connections and occasionally bask in the sunshine too.

Urban and rural communities alike have developed just such a range of actions and activities throughout all 2,000 years of Christian history, meaningful and positive interactions with and in the wider landscape. This book gathers such materials together as an aid to nurturing this deep-seated and popular instinct for outdoor worship. Wind and rain might seem a less attractive option than pew and nave at times, but it does no harm for Christians to get wet occasionally. Indeed there are many water-based rituals to be found that will enable just that.

So in the following pages are resources for the blessing of springs and reservoirs and the planting of a tree, for celebrating animals from hard-working bees to domestic pets, for giving thanks for the beauty of the meadows and the bounty of the sea, for shaping prayers beside a grave, for dispersing on a pilgrimage or gathering for an ecumenical picnic in a park. This book offers a wide selection of these and many other practices, and presents them as a resource to enable worshipping communities to continue this time-honoured and very public profession of the power of Christian ritual to connect and to heal. Surprising innovations and deep-rooted traditions alike are presented without agenda or hierarchy, other than to fire the imagination as to just how far the witness of the church can reach.

The very title of this book might seem a curious combination of words, if one considers 'liturgy' in its most formal sense. Yet the very word liturgy comes from a term meaning 'public service', the Greek words *litos ergos*, which by itself raises the prospect of wider engagement and visibility for liturgy than the more cloistered performance of a sacrament inside a church building might evoke. This book arises from work sponsored by the Susanna Wesley Foundation at Roehampton University, a university founded on three faith-based colleges. In parallel ways these institutions are also testament to the wider reach that church-based activity can have into the public domain, into academia and from there into the wide world of learning and research.

Other than celebrating the rich possibilities of liturgy to spill out once again into the landscape, this book has no particular agenda.

All the services have been used in the recent or distant past and are included without attempting to prove any particular theological point, or to foreground any one church tradition over another. We leave it up to the reader and their own church communities and leadership to decide which of the services would help to guide and inspire their own worship. And if any seem a challenge, there will be many others that offer opportunities, and no doubt inspiration, to continue to innovate and adapt again.

Bees and believers

It is debatable how far previous generations of Christians had any sort of 'environmental' sympathy in their outreach of Christian ritual to the natural world, at least in the sense we understand that today. But in a modern context where pollution, environmental damage, plastic waste and over-exploitation of resources are pressing matters for the church to address, these age-old traditions work just as well in focusing minds and readjusting priorities.

With that in mind, the first liturgy in this book has been chosen as an emblem of what can be done outdoors to inspire creative and positive action by a community of believers. It is a short blessing service for bees and beehives, drawn from the Russian Orthodox tradition and timeless in its application and beliefs. The service begins by focusing on the usefulness of bees to human needs, which could be a rather narrow motivation for environmental action, but like so many of the services in this book it widens its scope considerably to reflect on the place of the natural world in God's creation, on aesthetic as well as utilitarian values.

Installing a small bee house in a churchyard would be a small matter with very large significance, rather like the bees themselves given their importance as pollinators. Bee houses for gardens, often sold as 'bee hotels', are easy to find and need no maintenance once fixed in a suitable place, encouraging wild bees to come and make their homes inside. The Orthodox service suggests that bee blessings should be held annually on the Feast of St John the Baptist, 24 June, making the perfect midsummer event. As a way to demonstrate continuity between the life of the Christian community inside and outside the four walls of the church, there is little that could be easier to implement and explain. Planting some bee-friendly bushes in the churchyard would be an act of pastoral care as real as any other form of church outreach.

Perhaps more thought-provoking still in this bee liturgy and in other early services are urgent prayers to ward off unspecified harm caused by human action. In times gone by such harmful behaviour is often categorized in landscape liturgies as malevolent 'charms' or 'spells', something that one beekeeper might direct towards a neighbour, or as the simple theft of bees and any other agricultural produce. It takes no effort at all to broaden out the definition of such malign acts to encompass physical pollution, alongside these earlier concepts about spiritual contamination, and we have noted these points in our translations.

Reworking and repurposing liturgies for new challenges and situations is part of the lifeblood of the church's ritual life. Reading through the colourful, imaginative, creative and thought-provoking services in this book soon demonstrates just how far church ritual has continued to adapt over the centuries. So much of it is contextual, shaped around the concerns of any given community or culture. In that same spirit, it is therefore suggested that few of the following texts should be considered fixed, but rather a source of inspiration and infinite possibilities for adaptation to new situations and places. An Anglo-Saxon blessing for a contaminated natural spring might not seem like the most urgent of rituals to revive, but on closer examination would work just as well for any tainted or polluted body of natural water, which the modern world has in great abundance.

So this is a practical handbook, answering a modern need for liturgical resources connected to the environment. Church leaders and theologians have been vocal in urging communities to incorporate the natural world in their corporate worship in recent years, and this book provides attractive and authentic ways to achieve that. Outdoor rituals can also help to meet needs far broader than those of the church hierarchy, since they have innate appeal to many who might consider themselves 'spiritual but not religious'. At best they can offer a ritual language that helps communities make meaningful connections to the natural world, a meeting place that is open to all. The most public part of a parish church is not the interior but the landscape around it, hallowed turf sometimes referred to as God's acre, often with its own churchyard trees, and maybe a hedge and other planting that can be used to welcome bees and people alike.

The potential for reviving rituals lost for centuries has great popular appeal and local relevance, and generates interest from a local community in ways that a church-based service could not. These are time-honoured traditions in the main, rooted in historical precedent, but able to be revived in ways that resonate with current ecological concerns, providing a bridge between formal church life and a more diffuse sense of spirituality in nature. Seasons are marked, landmarks are celebrated, and the church can align itself closely with the needs and concerns of the people it cares for. Sometimes when it is difficult to bring people in to church, it might be easier to bring church to them.

Many books of nature-facing worship material have been published in recent years. In terms of animals, Professor Andrew Linzey has been leading in this field since the 1970s, and this book seeks to endorse and supplement such pioneering work with its counterparts found in older Christian tradition. Drawing on this rich church heritage greatly strengthens the credentials and authenticity of outdoor worship.

And finally it must be said that quite a lot of this will be seen as good fun. Some of the rituals will engage children in particular with activities in the outdoors, nurturing a sense of enchantment and wonder in the natural world. It would not be difficult to give a short talk beside a bee hotel in a churchyard or school's wild garden and bring to life some observations about the busy little inhabitants and their significance in the cycle of life.

This book emerged as a concept at a time when the coronavirus pandemic was still a distant threat, which meant that the notion of outdoor worship took on a new and sharper meaning as the churches were forced to close their doors. But the scale and scope of Christian ritual to engage creatively with God's creation offers far more than a short-term tactic and works in any place and time.

Pilgrims in the parish

A second motivation for producing this book is to help churches find old paths that connect people to place, that represent the best instincts and ambitions of a local community to hold things in common. The lingering power and appeal of folklore and landscape lore are well established as part of the cycle of rural life even today, popular expressions of ritual and custom that sometimes overlap closely with the life of the church. The seminal work on this topic is Professor Ronald Hutton's landmark book, *Stations of the Sun*, which offers an entertaining tour through a wide range of seasonal practices and their community celebrations.[1]

It was in compiling the section about Rogationtide processions, much explored in Professor Hutton's book, that gave one of the biggest insights into the nature of what outdoor worship was, is, and could be in the future. Today the Rogationtide is largely seen as an exercise in boundary walking, following and thereby affirming the limits of the parish, praying for a propitious year for all those who live and work within the designated area. As such it has certain shades of management and even ownership of the parish itself. It is often inter-

preted as a means of fixing the landmarks in popular memory, a way of marking borders in a time before maps. But to focus on this one aspect is to narrow down its scope considerably. The Rogation service as it is conceived today actually covers a multitude of virtues.

The first processions in the vicinity of a church in early Ireland and Britain were much more of a tour of sites of importance to the local community rather than any sort of interaction with boundaries, an exercise in visiting places of spiritual significance within the remit of any particular church community. As such that opens up a very wide range of the other liturgies in this book as suitable for a procession-ary ritual, visiting all manner of important community resources and memorials. It is certainly true that Rogation processions are largely seen through the lens of a tradition known as 'Beating the bounds', and there is undoubtedly a place for just such a witness today. But the possibilities are as large as the landscape itself, a tour of natural and built landmarks within a parish rests on ancient wisdom and custom.

In the early church these processions visited sites of what might be called sacred power, such as holy wells, ancient trees, stone crosses and places where significant events have occurred. So a Rogationtide pro-cession today could be framed in just such terms, a means of marking out places that are important to a modern community: bestowing a blessing on a recycling centre or a sports pitch, a reservoir or a bridge, a field or a hill. And indeed there are services for just such places found throughout this book.

In teasing those two aspects apart, boundary marking and visit-ing special community landmarks, one can open up an entire world of outdoor spirituality that offers something both new and exciting, but also very old and forgotten, a treasure buried in earliest Christian tradition. It is, if you like, a pilgrimage within the parish. As such it touches on a spiritual activity that seems to have remarkably enduring popular appeal, reaching people who might be less keen on formal church attendance. Parish pilgrimage is our summary of so much of what this book represents.

Renewal and inspiration

A curious aside in Acts 16 suggests that it was customary at the time of the early church for devout believers to assemble at riverbanks as places of worship, outside the city gates. The sequence takes place in Philippi, referring to a riverside location just outside the city gate which Paul assumed without explanation to be a likely place of worship. It turned out that he was right. He went there and met a woman called Lydia, whom he describes as 'a worshipper of God', which indicates that she was a gentile who was attracted to Judaism.

Further on in the passage it is clear that Paul makes repeated visits to this 'place of prayer' beside the river, after some of those using it had been converted to Christianity. Clearly he did not suggest it be abandoned, but rather adopted as his own place of mission. The text leaves open the distinct possibility that Lydia and her household were baptized in that same stretch of river, and indeed the site today now has a chapel to celebrate her baptism there. She is recognized as St Lydia of Thyatira.

Outdoor worship is particularly associated with periods of spiritual renewal and reform, from the missionary work of Paul, the desert sages of early monasticism, the travels of the Celtic Christians, clandestine meetings of early Lollards and the early energy of the Methodist movement, as previously mentioned. As a place of inspiration, of catching the spirit, the outdoors has a pivotal place in religious traditions of every kind. In Christian history one only needs to look at the wilderness mission of John the Baptist and his introduction of the first Christian sacrament – that same river baptism that Lydia underwent – to understand this trajectory from the city towards nature and its potential to precipitate far-reaching and radical change.

It is certainly true that not all of these various movements choosing to worship outdoors were driven by a deliberate decision to engage ritually in and with the natural world. The Celtic Christians in Britain are famed for their sympathy towards nature, but even for them it is difficult to claim with any certainty that this was a conscious expression of faith in terms that we can categorize as environmentalism. And in a way it is not necessary to understand the motives to draw inspiration from the consequences.

We know relatively little about the performance of Celtic liturgy, yet there is one intriguing aside describing the first worshipping community on Iona. St Columba, we are told, 'entered the church as usual on the Lord's day after the Gospel had been read' in order to conduct the Eucharist.[2] From this aside we learn that the Gospel was habitually read outdoors, that the most solemn service of the church clearly began in the open air. History does not record why they did this. Perhaps the building was too small for all of the gathered to hear the readings and prayers, so they would file in later to take Communion. Or perhaps the community felt that there was a particular resonance to be found in proclaiming the Gospel to the widest possible audience. We do not know for sure, but the famed sensitivity of Celtic spirituality towards nature was no doubt embellished by just such practices, a point that is developed briefly at the end of this introduction.

Another of the church's great outdoor evangelists is St Francis of Assisi. Most people know that he famously preached to the birds, but what is less well known is that this event was the first thing he did after deciding between life as a contemplative hermit or life as an active witness to society. For whatever reason, therefore, it seems best to describe this impulse to take Christianity out into the streets as a fundamentally missionary action, a hallmark of a pioneering phase of a church community's life.

And like all such reforming church movements, it tends to go into decline as the church becomes settled and established. For all their fabled travelling and outdoor preaching, it wasn't long before John and Charles Wesley were encouraging the establishment of their own buildings, a network of chapels across the country. Communal prayer life in the Methodist community gathered once again under a roof. The binary of church and street was soon domesticated to become a binary of church and chapel.

Just a generation after the Wesley brothers died, some in the Methodist Church were growing restless at the settled nature of worship and proposed a revival based on large-scale outdoor meetings, partly an extension of the love-feast gatherings which have their own chapter in this book. The Wesleyan Conference in 1807 was emphatic in its refusal.[3] And so a new church movement was born, the Primitive Methodists, characterized by outdoor gatherings known as camp meetings. Needless to say, not many years passed before the Primitive Methodists were building their own network of chapels and moving their meetings quietly indoors. Fortunately, outdoor Methodist worship continued to flourish in the more favourable climate of America, the camp meeting becoming a staple of Christian worship, serving as a prototype that developed into the modern-day church festival. Gatherings such as Greenbelt, Spring Harvest and New Wine arguably reflect an ongoing legacy of this outdoor worship tradition back in the UK, albeit with varying amounts of exposure to the British weather.

'A man or woman might better praye in the field than in the cherche of God,' wrote a pair of medieval dissenters in 1460, Thomas and Agnes Cole, who were followers of John Wyclif.[4] The notion that the great outdoors could be 'better' than a church is a topic for discussion elsewhere, but what is clearly true is that landscape spirituality brings a bracing breeze to established religion, both literally and metaphorically.

The enthusiasm with which some of the repressed Covenanting dissenters in Scotland took to the fields is palpable, following the imposition of a more hierarchical church order after Cromwell's defeat of the Scottish army in 1651. The Covenanters even began to view their meeting places in the landscape as somehow set apart by nature, contrived at the creation of the world itself as naturally given over to prayer and meeting. 'Amidst the lonely mountains, we remembered the words of our Lord, that true worship was not peculiar to Jerusalem or Samaria; that the beauty of holiness consisted not in consecrated buildings, or material temples,' wrote the memorably named John Blackadder in the seventeenth century. What is particularly striking is that his is such a thoroughly Protestant voice, this is no proponent of pilgrimage or nature spirituality.[5] And to balance this we can look at Roman Catholic practice even today, where there is a host of well-considered and meaningful worship material, some reproduced in this book, which fixes Christian worship as firmly in the outdoors as any of the reformers achieved. The landscape is far bigger and more accommodating than any of our human attempts to compartmentalize it, closer to the divine in that respect than the human.

So many of the great movements in Christian tradition have found their feet quite literally by heading out of the buildings, even out of the towns altogether, and into the wider world.

Celtic land exorcism and consecration

No British book of landscape liturgies would be complete without acknowledging the power of Celtic Christian tradition, a romantic aura still lingering at numerous sites in the landscape today. Yet for all their famed love of nature, the actual rituals the early Celtic missionaries directed towards their environment would be relatively difficult to recreate in a modern context. Marked by intensity and solitude, lonely vigils on the seashore and long days spent fasting on mountains and in wild places, they do not exactly commend themselves to a modern congregation or to communal worship.[6] However there are certain principles that could be adapted to work. Many of the rituals directed towards nature were essentially a way of incorporating the patterns and concerns of the changing seasons and unpredictable weather into the church calendar and its daily cycle of prayers and rituals.

Celtic spirituality was also highly sensitive to the need to demarcate sacred areas in the landscape. The Welsh term *llan-* appears at the start of many place names and is actually a word used to describe not a church but the enclosure around an area of sacred land, usually circular. The sites so blessed were subsequently used for the foundation of a church, a cleansing exercise that was a precondition for a church's consecration. The church historian Sabine Baring-Gould describes the ritual landscape cleansing thus:

> It was customary for a holy man or woman who desired to found a *llan*, to go to the spot and continue there for forty days and nights; during all that time it was incumbent on him to eat nothing save a morsel of bread and an egg, and to drink only milk and water, and that once in the day. The Sundays were excepted. This done, the place was regarded as consecrated for ever.[7]

One such sacred enclave in the landscape was set apart by great missionary St Cedd, who founded a monastery at Lastingham in North Yorkshire in the seventh century. His ritual preparation of the land was recorded by the church historian the Venerable Bede, and is the basis for the above description. But this summary misses one important aspect: St Cedd consecrated the land during the season of Lent, the landscape redeemed by being woven into the church calendar. When summoned to speak to the king before the 40 days were up, a fellow monk took over and fasted on site in Cedd's place. Bede also quotes Isaiah chapter 35, which talks about nature flourishing in the wilderness, tying this redemption of the land directly into biblical tradition and language about the Holy Land. This is a rare and important piece of Celtic landscape lore that involved more than simply fasting.

This Celtic ritual of seventh-century Britain shows remarkable consistency with a similar landscape exorcism and consecration performed many thousands of miles away in the late fifth century. The abbot St Sabas spent the whole of Lent in prayer on the hill of Castellium, a disused Roman-era fortress in the Judean desert, about 16 km to the east of Jerusalem. St Sabas anointed the land with consecrated oil and then fasted and prayed for 40 days until the demons were expelled and he could found a church and monastery.[8]

There are certainly processional walks in the early British church that are bounding rituals which circumscribe sacred space. Several records talk of animals taking part in such rituals, nature itself involved in setting apart a site as special. Celtic lore describes how St Patrick was led by an angel as he walked around the circular boundary for his new monastic centre at Armagh. It remains to this day the ecclesiastical capital of Ireland, demonstrating the lingering power of landscape liturgies. Yet for all the significance of this path there is no evidence that subsequent generations at Armagh ever undertook any sort of repeat procession around this boundary.[9] The sanctification of an area of land was more of a one-off ritual at the foundation of a holy site, as practised by St Cedd and St Sabas, rather than an annual public boundary walk.

Circumambulations are an important form of ecclesiastical ritual and certainly become a powerful motif in the later medieval church, which brings us back to the Rogationtide practice of beating the bounds, as described above. But care must be taken here not to backward project these parish boundary ceremonies on to a period when there were no parishes.

It is a point that bears repeating by way of conclusion: the earliest Rogationtide processions in Britain were not about marking boundaries but rather about visiting periphery sacred sites such as holy wells, blessing the fields for a successful harvest, and warding off harm.[10] As the chapter on Rogation and parish liturgies explains in its introduction, the Rogation was first introduced in Vienne in south-west France by the city's bishop St Mamertus in the late fifth century.

Cautious as any theologian should be about the risks of introducing a new form of Christian ritual, Mamertus originally picked an inconspicuous church on the edge of the city in order to test his procession as quietly as possible. He need not have worried. From the very start the procession attracted great enthusiasm from the local people, who joined in and helped to cement its place in popular tradition. It was not long before Rogationtide was being celebrated across the whole of Europe.

There is much in this book that can serve as a meeting point for the church and the people in the streets, parks, shores and fields. It celebrates that most powerful instinct for the church to spread its wings, to catch that same breeze that once swayed John beside the River Jordan.

ANIMAL BLESSINGS

For many of us animals are the closest relationship we have to the natural world. Constant companions and very much part of home life, pets in particular have a special place in our hearts, much cherished and loved, and much mourned at their deaths. The liturgies in this chapter offer a way of channelling such emotions and connections. But they also look beyond, to a celebration of all of God's creatures for their own sake, rather than serving human needs alone.

Bees in particular are an important part of many ecosystems, infinitely greater than their immediate use to humans, and are rightly honoured here with their own thoughtfully composed liturgy from the Russian Orthodox tradition. It is one of the hopes of this book that it will inspire and enable churches to adopt their own little bee home in a churchyard wherever possible, offering sanctuary and an honoured place to our beloved and much-threatened pollinators.

It is not difficult to find meaningful animal interactions in the Gospel accounts of Jesus, from the very moment of his birth in the stable through to his observations and comments about bird life. Jesus compared himself favourably to animals, a mother hen and the lamb of God, and was also touched by a dove at the moment of his baptism. 'You save humans and animals alike, O LORD', sang the psalmist – just one of many Jewish verses which ground such attitudes in wise and ancient traditions (Ps. 36.6).

The spiritual significance of animals is a theme picked up from the early church onwards, with hymns, poems and prayers abounding in inspiration sparked by contact with the natural world. The early Christian writer Origen argued that animals would share in the universal redemption.[11] That is not to say the whole of Christian history has been marked by a sympathy towards all of God's creatures, and indeed Origen's writings have been contested, and humans considered to be superior in a hierarchical order of creation.

Indeed many theologians have taught that the natural world was provided as a resource for humans to exploit. Such a line of thinking had fewer worrying consequences in medieval times, when much of the world was still wilderness, and wolves and bears might easily provoke uncharitable thoughts towards nature in the raw. Today however the effects of human over-exploitation and environmental degradation have given a new urgency to the work of theologians alongside others in re-evaluating the ethical, moral and spiritual aspects of our relationship to our fellow creatures.

Modern theologians have picked up this important thread and continue to witness to the spiritual and devotional significance of animals in a number of ways. Revd Barbara Allen, former chaplain at the Lort Smith Animal Hospital in Melbourne, has kindly provided a blessing service to be held on St Francis Day, 4 October. Professor Andrew Linzey has a particularly venerable place in the development of animal theology, having produced books on the subject since the 1970s. He is founder and director of the Oxford Centre for Animal Ethics[12] and has also contributed two liturgies to this chapter. His influence has helped to inspire other contributors, including another Oxford-based charity, Pan-Orthodox Concern for Animals (panorthodoxconcernforanimals. org).

This book envisions that the blessing services involving animals are conducted outdoors. For animal welfare issues around bringing pets into a church building, some simple but important considerations need to be borne in mind. Among many good resources on this topic we recommend Professor Linzey's book *Animal Rites*.[13]

Blessing of the Bees and Hives

The following prayer and ritual is a traditional Russian Orthodox prayer for the blessing of bees and the thriving of their hives.
It involves the sprinkling of holy water over the hives three times, a
reading from Luke's Gospel and a blessing on the keepers who maintain the bee communities.[14] At the end of this ritual, the prayers seek
to dispel 'spells' or 'enchantments' that may linger around the bees, a
term we have translated as 'pollution' for reasons both spiritual and
environmental. Thus the service begins by describing bees as useful for
our needs, but ends by speaking of human contamination; a balanced
view of our place in creation.

The Bee Blessing

The minister and congregation gather near the beehive

Minister: Blessed is your name, Father, Son and Holy
　　　　　Spirit, now and forever.

All:　　　**Amen.**

　　　　　Holy God, holy and mighty, holy and immortal, have
　　　　　mercy on us. (*Said three times*)
　　　　　All-holy Trinity have mercy on us. O Lord cleanse away
　　　　　our sins, O Master, forgive our iniquities, O holy one visit
　　　　　and heal our infirmities, for your name's sake.
　　　　　Lord have mercy. (*Said three times*)
　　　　　Glory to the Father and to the Son and to the Holy Spirit
　　　　　both now and forever unto the ages of ages.

The Lord's Prayer

Lord have mercy. (*Said 12 times*)

O come let us worship God our king. O come let us worship and fall down before Christ, our King and God. O come let us worship and fall down before the very Christ, our King and God.

Psalm 50

During the recitation of the psalm the minister blesses the beehive once with holy water; two further blessings will follow later in the service

The mighty one, God the LORD,
speaks and summons the earth
from the rising of the sun to its setting.
Out of Zion, the perfection of beauty,
God shines forth.

Our God comes and does not keep silence,
before him is a devouring fire,
and a mighty tempest all around him.
He calls to the heavens above
and to the earth, that he may judge his people:

'Gather to me my faithful ones,
who made a covenant with me by sacrifice!'
The heavens declare his righteousness,
for God himself is judge.

'Hear, O my people, and I will speak,
O Israel, I will testify against you.
I am God, your God.'
'Not for your sacrifices do I rebuke you;
your burnt-offerings are continually before me.'

'I will not accept a bull from your house,
or goats from your folds.'
'For every wild animal of the forest is mine,
the cattle on a thousand hills.'

'I know all the birds of the air,
and all that moves in the field is mine.'
'If I were hungry, I would not tell you,
for the world and all that is in it is mine.'

'Do I eat the flesh of bulls,
or drink the blood of goats?'
**'Offer to God a sacrifice of thanksgiving,
and pay your vows to the Most High.'**

'Call on me in the day of trouble;
I will deliver you, and you shall glorify me.'
**But to the wicked God says:
'What right have you to recite my statutes,
or take my covenant on your lips?'**

'For you hate discipline,
and you cast my words behind you.'
**'You make friends with a thief when you see one,
and you keep company with adulterers.'**

'You give your mouth free rein for evil,
and your tongue frames deceit.'
**'You sit and speak against your kin;
you slander your own mother's child.'**

'These things you have done and I have been silent;
you thought that I was one just like yourself.
But now I rebuke you, and lay the charge before you.'
**'Mark this, then, you who forget God,
or I will tear you apart, and there will be no one to deliver.'**

'Those who bring thanksgiving as their sacrifice honour me;
to those who go the right way
I will show the salvation of God.'

Let us pray to the Lord.
Lord have mercy.

Blessing prayer one

O God Creator of all, who blesses seed and causes it to multiply
and makes it suitable for our use: through the intercessions of the
Forerunner John the Baptist, mercifully hearing our prayers, be
pleased to bless and sanctify these bees by your own deep mercy, that
they may abundantly bear fruit for the beauty and decoration of your
temple and your holy altars, as well as being useful for us, in Christ
Jesus our Lord, to whom be honour and glory unto the ages of ages.
Amen.

Blessing prayer two

O God, who knows how to benefit humans and dumb animals alike in their labours, in your loving mercy you taught us to employ even the fruits and works of the bees for our needs. We humbly pray to you, the Almighty: bless these bees and multiply them, preserving them and making them abundant. May everyone who works and cares for these living creatures, hoping in your power and in your unending bounty, be worthy to receive abundant fruits from their labours and be filled with heavenly blessings, in Christ Jesus our Lord, to whom be honour and glory unto the ages of ages. Amen.

The minister blesses the beehive with holy water for the second time

Gospel reading: Luke 24.36–44

While they were talking about this, Jesus himself stood among them and said to them, 'Peace be with you.' They were startled and terrified, and thought that they were seeing a ghost. He said to them, 'Why are you frightened, and why do doubts arise in your hearts? Look at my hands and my feet; see that it is I myself. Touch me and see; for a ghost does not have flesh and bones as you see that I have.' And when he had said this, he showed them his hands and his feet. While in their joy they were disbelieving and still wondering, he said to them, 'Have you anything here to eat?' They gave him a piece of broiled fish, and he took it and ate in their presence.

Then he said to them, 'These are my words that I spoke to you while I was still with you – that everything written about me in the law of Moses, the prophets, and the psalms must be fulfilled.'

Blessing prayer three

After reading the Gospel, the minister says:

By the power of the words of the Gospel may we be cleansed of our sins, may all pollution that is in this place be destroyed and perished, and may the blessing of Almighty God, Father, Son and Holy Spirit be upon it.
Amen.

The minister sprinkles the beehive with holy water for a third time and then all take their leave

The Prayer of St Mammes for Animals

This prayer is attributed to one of the earliest saints in this book, the martyr St Mammes of Caesarea, who lived in the mid-third century and was executed during persecutions under the Emperor Aurelian. St Mammes had been orphaned by the death of his parents, who had also been arrested because of their faith. He miraculously escaped an execution attempt as a young man and went to live on a mountain near Caesarea, in the north-east of modern-day Israel, where he befriended a lion and would milk wild animals to help feed the poor. His power over animals was such that when a second attempt was made to kill him in AD 275 he was thrown to wild beasts which refused to attack him, leading to his eventual execution by trident. Tradition records that his relics were taken to France and placed in the cathedral dedicated to him at Langres, in the east of the country.

Such harmonious living in and with the natural world was deeply rooted in St Mammes's faith, and indeed he makes a connection in this very prayer between the suffering of animals and the sin of a fallen world. The prayer was attributed to St Mammes after his death and given in a vision to one of his devotees, beginning with a short introduction explaining how he came to recite this intercession. This text is reproduced with kind permission from the resources of the Pan-Orthodox Concern for Animals, whose details are listed in the introduction to this chapter, and has been very slightly adapted so all can say this ancient prayer first spoken by St Mammes.

The Prayer of St Mammes for Animals

Behold, I, the sinner and lowest one Mammes, dwelling in the mountains and through the power of our Lord Jesus Christ milked deer and made cheese, distributing to the poor, and walking through the mountains and caves until my death. There when I was passing through, approached John and Philotheos, who entreated me saying: 'The wrath of the devil has fallen upon our flocks and herdsmen and they are dying terribly. We pray you, O saint of God, pray for them, that they might be healed from every evil, in memory of the age to come, and to the glory of God.' I then said to them: 'My spiritual brothers, I am a sinner, and God does not listen to sinners.' But they persisted in entreating me. Hearkening, then, to their prayers, I pray to the Lord, saying:

> I call upon you, our Lord Jesus Christ, the true God, who descended from the Father's bosom, and was incarnate of the Holy Mother of God, and ever-virgin Mary, willingly enduring the cross and death, and rose on the third day, granting life to the race of mortals. Hearken to me the sinner, your unworthy servant, and all those whose spirits are spent and who are in great trouble, who call upon your name. O Lord our God, remember the name of your servant St Mammes and do not allow the flocks or the herds of their animals to be afflicted by diabolical influence or any other sickness.

> Yes, O Lord our God, who made the heaven and the earth, and whose word grants all things towards salvation to our people, do not neglect this my prayer, from your humble and lowest servant; but hearken to me, O Lord who loves all humans, and to this my prayer when read, whether for a flock, or oxen, or mules. Do not let sickness or other temptation come close to these animals, that being always guarded by you, we might offer up glory and worship to the Father and to the Son and to the Holy Spirit, now and ever and unto the ages of ages. Amen.

Blessing of the Animals on St Francis Day

Many famous Christians have witnessed to the need for animal welfare over the centuries. This thoughtfully composed liturgy suggests mentioning their work as a way of underscoring how deep and long these traditions have endured. Among those whose voices have been included are St Francis of Assisi, on whose feast day, 4 October, this service can be held; John Wesley, founder of the Methodist Church; Anna Sewell, devout Quaker and author of *Black Beauty*; and Meister Eckhart, a fourteenth-century mystic and theologian from Germany.

The liturgy was written by Revd Barbara Allen, former chaplain at the Lort Smith Animal Hospital in Melbourne, minister in the Uniting Church in Australia, and author of *Animals in Religion*.[15] It has been designed for outdoor use and encourages participants either to bring along their pet animal or a photograph of them. It could also be held at a farm, and with the participation of an animal charity such as the RSPCA, the RSPB, or local nature conservancy group. Any animals in the environs during the service, such as birds or squirrels, can also be noted during the proceedings and blessings. The service is intended to be a public expression of the bond humans have with animals. Through the service participants are able to make them an integral part of their worship life and relationships.

In terms of blessing animals, the liturgy's author notes that in the Scriptures the act of blessing means 'the imparting of power or life'. The person performing the blessing is mediating that power from God or Christ to the person or animal involved. To bless is more than an expression of goodwill or caring: to bless is to impart God's power in person. The blessing of each animal, by name, means that health, healing and life are being mediated from God for the benefit of the animal in its relationship with its human partners. *Shalom* is one such Hebrew expression of blessing.

The Blessing of the Animals

Minister: 'The moral progress of a nation and its greatness should be judged by the way it treats its animals.' (Mahatma Gandhi, 1869–1948)

Call to worship

Minister: We worship with the creatures we love.

Reading: Job 12.7, 8b, 10a

'But ask the animals, and they will teach you; the birds of the air, and they will tell you; … and the fish of the sea will declare to you. In his hand is the life of every living thing …'
All: Amen.

Silence

Introit

Reading based on Genesis chapter 1

God said, 'Let the waters bring forth swarms of living creatures, and let birds fly above the earth across the dome of the sky.' So God created the great sea monsters and every living creature that moves, of every kind, with which the waters swarm, and every winged bird of every kind. And God saw that it was good. And God blessed them.

And God said, 'Let the earth bring forth living creatures of every kind, cattle and creeping things and wild animals of the earth of every kind.' And it was so. And God saw that it was good.

Then God said, 'Let us make humankind'. And God blessed them. God saw everything that had been made, and indeed, it was very good.

Opening prayer/processional

Come, let us gather together.
Let us join the gathering: we bring fins and feathers.

Come, all is ready for all of creation.
Let us join the gathering: we bring scales and fur.

Come let us praise our Creator.
We are loved: we bring skin.

Come, with fins, feathers, scales, fur and skin. As we gather, we are mindful that, as part of God's creation, we wish the best for one another. Within this faith community we express this in prayer, and through blessing. Let us pass God's blessing among one another: Peace be with you!
And also with you.

The exchanging of the peace, extending to the animals

Hymn

Minister: Let us sing together.

> *Suggested hymn choices include:* 'All people that on earth do dwell', 'Morning has Broken', *or* 'All things bright and beautiful'

Prayers of Adoration, Thanksgiving and Confession

'If the Creator and Father of every living thing is rich in mercy towards all – if he does not overlook or despise any of the works of his own hands, if he desires even the meanest of them to be happy according to their degree – how is it that such a complication of evils oppresses, yea, overwhelms them?' (John Wesley, *Sermon 60 'The General Deliverance'*)

Minister: Creator God, You have made a beautiful world filled with wonder and surprises!
All: **We adore you.**

Creator God who has gifted us with the blessing of animals, those in the wild, those on farms, those in our own homes,
We adore you.

Creator God, you brought into being that which we could not imagine for ourselves, life we cannot see without the aid of microscopes, animals we can only see in pictures from remote regions of this planet earth,
We adore you.

We thank you for abundant life; for the birds we hear in the morning, for the drone of the bees when we are outside, for the vast tapestry of life which is interwoven,
We give you thanks.

We thank you for the gift of our own animal companions. For the joy they bring us, for the unconditional love and forgiveness which teach us about you; for the confidant, the listener, the stress-releaser, for the benefits they are to our health and to our spirit.
We give you thanks.

And yet we know that we have not always been faithful caretakers of our animals. Forgive us when we have dirtied their environment, erased places of shelter, polluted the waters, killed off their food supplies or neglected to feed or tend animals in our own communities.
Forgive us when we have neglected our own animal companions; when we have said we are too busy to play with them, when we have shooed them away; when we have made excuses, saying we are too tired ... too busy ... more important engagements have come up ... so that we do not walk them, cuddle them, spend time with them.
Forgive us.

Forgive us when we have not loved them as they have loved us. Forgive us when we have not considered the wider picture; when we have neglected the animals in the wild, the cruelty inflicted in the name of 'sport', or in the name of food production.
Forgive us when we have focused only on our 'favourites' and neglected the care of the supposedly less beautiful, those who hold a lower public profile.
Each year more animals are becoming extinct, or are added to the endangered species list: forgive us, for allowing beauty to be forever destroyed.
Forgive us when we neglect to see all animals as part of your creation, forgive us when we neglect to acknowledge that your love beats in all hearts, and that you give breath to all creation.

God is love. Through Christ your sins are forgiven. Take hold of this forgiveness, and live your life, knowing that you are forgiven, and deeply loved. Know that the Holy Spirit will enable you to live fully, richly and deeply.
Amen.

Reading: Psalm 104.24–25, 27–28, 30–31

O Lord, how manifold are your works!
In wisdom you have made them all;
the earth is full of your creatures.
Yonder is the sea, great and wide,
creeping things innumerable are there,
living things both small and great …

These all look to you
to give them their food in due season;
when you give to them, they gather it up;
when you open your hand, they are filled with good things …

When you send forth your spirit, they are created;
and you renew the face of the ground.
May the glory of the Lord endure forever.

Reading: Matthew 6.25–26

'Therefore I tell you, do not worry about your life, what you will eat
or what you will drink, or about your body, what you will wear. Is
not life more than food, and the body more than clothing? Look at
the birds of the air; they neither sow nor reap nor gather into barns,
and yet your heavenly Father feeds them. Are you not of more value
than they?'
This is the word of the Lord.
Thanks be to God.

Reflection/sermon

'Apprehend God in all things, for God is in all things. Every single
creature is full of God, and is a book about God. Every creature is a
word of God. If I spent enough time with the tiniest creature, even a
caterpillar – I would never have to prepare a sermon so full of God is
every creature.' (Meister Eckhart, *c.*1260–1328)

Hymn

The suggested hymn is based on the Prayer of St Francis: 'Make me
a channel of your peace'

Offering

'What right have they to torment and disfigure God's creatures? He said cruelty was the devil's own trademark, and if we saw any one who took pleasure in cruelty we might know who he belonged to, for the devil was a murderer from the beginning, and a tormentor to the end.' (Anna Sewell, *Black Beauty*)

It is suggested that a portion of the offering could go towards an animal cause, or as a donation to a local animal shelter. Donations of dog and cat food could be placed in a basket at the door of the church/worship space, and brought forward as part of the offering. Many food banks in the UK collect and distribute pet food.

Prayers of intercession

Intercessor: Loving God, we bring to you the prayers of the people. Today we offer up prayers for those involved in animal welfare and conservation work: for the RSPCA, for A Rocha, for the World Wide Fund for Nature, for Tearfund, and (*name local conservation and animal welfare services*).
Amen.

We pray for those who are working at policy and project levels, and for those tending to the needs of animals.
Amen.

We pray for farmers, that the animals in their care are treated with dignity and respect.
Amen.

We pray for the strays on our streets; help us not to turn away, but to bring them to a place of safety, where they can be fed, given medical treatment, and the chance to find a loving home.
Amen.

Help us to be generous: with money, time, and the offer of hospitality within our homes.
Amen.

We pray for vets and vet practices: enable your wisdom and compassion to be evident wherever there are sick or dying animals. Enable the animals to sense your presence.
Amen.

Comfort grieving owners; allow the many warm memories to break the frost of grief.
Amen.

The Lord's Prayer

Blessing of the animals

Some churches have the animals line up in order to be blessed, but this can add stress to the service. It is suggested that the minister/worship leader should circulate, asking the name of the animal, placing their hand on the animal's head (if appropriate) and then saying the blessing. If a person has brought a photograph of the animal rather than the animal itself, then bless the owner, and have them pass on this blessing when they return home.

Minister: *(state name)*, you were created by God, and you are loved by God. May you and your human family experience joy and companionship together, and continue to be a blessing to each other.

In the name of the Father, Son and Holy Spirit.
Amen.

Remembrance of those who have died

We remember our animal companions who are no longer with us physically.
We give thanks for the gifts they gave us and the variety of ways they enriched and blessed our lives.
We are confident that our Creator continues to care for them.
Amen.

Hymn

The suggested hymn is based on a poem by St Francis: 'All creatures of our God and King'

Blessing and dismissal

A prayer by Norman Habel, Old Testament and ecological scholar:

**God, our Creator, help us to love all creatures as kin, all animals as
partners on earth, all birds as messengers of praise, all minute beings
as expressions of your mysterious design, and all frogs as voices
of hope.**
Amen.

Go out into the world, love one another.
Cherish your animal family, protest against abuse and neglect of
our animals; exercise stewardship of all creation, so that all can
experience God's Shalom.
Go out into the world, my horizontal and vertical brothers and sisters
in Christ.
In the name of the Father, Son and Holy Spirit.
Amen.

St Bride's Charm for Animal Blessings

Charm is an apt word to describe this touching little prayer. It is a blessing for horses and farm animals which invokes the name of St Brigid of Kildare ('Bride'), who was famous for the charms she wove over animals and agricultural produce. This blessing is included in the extensive collection of oral traditions from the Gaelic-speaking Highlands and Islands gathered and translated by the Scottish writer Alexander Carmichael, which he called the *Carmina Gadelica*.[16]

St Bride's Charm

The charm put by Bride the beneficent,
On her goats, on her sheep, on her kine [cows],
On her horses, on her chargers, on her herds,
Early and late going home, and from home.

To keep them from rocks and ridges.
From the heels and the horns of one another.
From the birds of the Red Rock,
And from Luath of the Feinne.

From the blue peregrine hawk of Creag Duilion,
From the brindled eagle of Ben-Ard,
From the swift hawk of Tordun,
From the surly raven of Bard's Creag.

From the fox of the wiles,
From the wolf of the Mam,
From the foul-smelling pole-cat,
And from the restless great-hipped bear.

From every hoofed of four feet.
And from every hatched of two wings.

Liturgies of Animal Care

Celebrating the creatures and a service for animal welfare

The following two liturgies have been written by one of the leading theologians on animals and human relationships with the natural world. Professor Andrew Linzey is director of the Oxford Centre for Animal Ethics and has produced a number of groundbreaking books on this subject.[17]

Introducing this first liturgy of 'Celebrating the creatures', Professor Linzey stresses that celebrating creation should not be confused with deifying it, that is, treating it as God. Creation is in a fallen state, incomplete and imperfect, and this liturgy reflects an eschatological hope in its consummation in Christ, the new creation promised in 2 Corinthians 5.17. He also makes a direct connection between the celebration and preservation of our fellow creatures:

> there is a direct relationship between our inability to celebrate animals and our dismal record of exploitation. We should not be surprised if we exploit our fellow creatures if we do not know how to celebrate, rejoice, and give thanks for the beautiful world God has made. If we treat the world as trash it may be because so many people imagine the world as just that.[18]

The second liturgy, 'An order of service for animal welfare', marks an important milestone in the development of modern nature-facing liturgies, since it is based on a text created for the RSPCA in 1975. Revised versions of this service have been in use ever since, commonly held on 4 October to mark the World Day for Animals and the Feast of St Francis of Assisi. Professor Linzey points out that the RSPCA was founded in 1824 by an Anglican priest, Revd Arthur Broome, with a distinctly Christian sense of purpose, a way of extending charity and benevolence towards all of God's creatures.

The Oxford Centre for Animal Ethics is online at:
www.oxfordanimalethics.com.

1 Celebrating the Creatures

Minister: We have come together to rejoice with God the Creator at
the wonderful creation around us.

O God, you love all things that exist: and despise none of
the things which you have made, for you would have made
nothing you didn't love. You spare all things, for they are
yours – O Lord who loves the living. For your immortal
Spirit is in all things. (Wisd. 11.24–25, 26–12.1)

All: **Let us sing to the Lord
a new song:
a song for all
the creatures of the earth.**

Let us rejoice
in the goodness of God
shown in the beauty
of little things.
**Let us marvel
at the little creatures
who are innocent
in God's sight.**

Let us extol
God's handiwork
in the complexity
of their lives.
**Let us not be haughty or proud
too full of ourselves
to praise the Lord
of little things.**

Let us rejoice
in the other worlds
sublime and mysterious
that God has made.
The world of earthworms
burrowing in the ground.

The world of skylarks
soaring above us.
The world of foxes
playing around their dens.

Let us hear
the divine rejoicing
throughout the whole earth:
'the earth is mine
and the fullness thereof' (Ps. 24.1, ESV).

First reading: Psalm 104.24, 28b–30

O LORD, how manifold are your works!
In wisdom you have made them all;
the earth is full of your creatures.
When you open your hand, they are filled with good things.
When you hide your face, they are dismayed;
when you take away their breath, they die and return to their dust.
When you send forth your spirit, they are created;
and you renew the face of the ground.

Prayer

Help us to wonder, Lord,
to stand in awe;
to stand and stare;
and so to praise you
for the richness of the world
you have laid before us.

God of the universe, all creatures praise you:
the sun setting on the lake,
the birds flying upward towards the heavens;
the growl of the bear,
the darting of the stickleback;
the purring of the cat,

the wide eyes of the tiger;
the swift legs of the cheetah,
the dance of the hare;
the lapping of the dog,
the descent of the dove.
God of a thousand ears,
the music of your creatures
resounds throughout creation,
and in heaven a symphony is made.
Help us to wonder, Lord,
to stand in awe;
to stand and stare;
and so to praise you
for the richness of the world
you have laid before us.

Second reading from the writings of St Athanasius

[The Logos] extends [its] power everywhere, illuminating all things
visible and invisible, containing and enclosing them in [itself], [giving]
life and everything, everywhere, to each individually and to all
together creating an exquisite single euphonious harmony.

There follows a period of silence

Christ in all things,
restore our senses
and give us again
that experience of joy
in all created things.

Christ in all things;
in the waves breaking on the shore;
in the beauty of the sunset;
in the fragrant blossom of spring;
in the music that makes our hearts dance;
in the kisses of embracing love;
in the cries of the innocent.
Christ in all things,
restore our senses
and give us again
that experience of joy
in all created things.

Large and immense God,
help us to know the littleness
of our lives without you;
the littleness of our thoughts
without your inspiration;
and the littleness of our hearts
without your love;
you are God beyond our littleness
yet in one tiny space and time
you became one of us
and all those specks of dust
you love for all eternity;
enlarge our hearts and minds
to reverence all living things
and in our care for them
to become big with your grace
and signs of your kingdom.

A prayer to God the Holy Spirit

Heavenly dove,
descend on us we pray
and in your flight
reunite our sinful wills
to your heavenly will
so we may soar upwards
and see the smallness
of ourselves amid the vastness
of your unfolding creation. Amen.
**We look forward
with all your creatures
to the wonderful consummation
of all things in Christ
when death and pain
shall be no more
and the whole earth
shall unite with those
in heaven and
praise your name, saying:
Worthy are you**

our Lord and God
to receive glory
and honour and power
for you created all things
and by your will
they were created
and have their being. (Rev. 4.11, ESV)

God of manifold blessings,
source of all that is good
and true and holy,
raise us up to see
the world through your eyes
so that we may treasure
each blessed creature
alive with your Spirit
and touched by your creative hand;
and may the blessing of
this wonderful God
Creator, Redeemer and Sanctifier
be upon us,
now and forever,
Amen.

2 A Service for Animal Welfare

One or more of the following sentences may be said:

In the beginning, God created the heavens and the earth. (Gen. 1.1, ESV)

God saw everything that he had made, and indeed, it was very good. (Gen. 1.31)

I will remember my covenant that is between me and you and every living creature of all flesh; and the waters shall never again become a flood to destroy all flesh. (Gen. 9.15)

You save humans and animals alike, O LORD. (Ps. 36.6)

They will not hurt or destroy on all my holy mountain; for the earth will be full of the knowledge of the Lord as the waters cover the sea. (Isa. 11.9)

Are not five sparrows sold for two pennies? Yet not one of them is forgotten in God's sight. (Luke 12.6)

For the creation waits with eager longing for the revealing of the children of God; for the creation was subjected to futility, not of its own will but by the will of the one who subjected it, in hope that the creation itself will be set free from its bondage to decay and will obtain the freedom of the glory of the children of God. (Rom. 8.19–21)

Minister: Almighty God,
          we come together
          to thank you
          for the beauty and glory of your creation;
          to praise you
          for your holiness and grace;

to acknowledge our responsibility to animals
and for our use of the created world.
But, first of all, we pray for your forgiveness
because of our part in sins of thoughtlessness
and cruelty towards animal life.

A pause for reflection may follow

All: **Almighty God,**
you have given us
temporary lordship
of your beautiful creation.
But we have misused our power,
turned away from responsibility
and marred your image in us.
Forgive us, true Lord,
especially for our callousness
and cruelty to animals.
Help us to follow the way
of your Son, Jesus Christ,
who expressed power in humility
and lordship in loving service.
Enable us, by your Spirit,
to walk in newness of life,
healing injury, avoiding wrong
and making peace with all your creatures.

God of everlasting love,
who is eternally forgiving:
pardon and restore us,
and make us one with you
in your new creation.
Amen.

First reading

Either (a):
In the beginning when God created the heavens and the earth, the
earth was a formless void and darkness covered the face of the deep,
while a wind from God swept over the face of the waters.
And God said, 'Let the earth bring forth living creatures of every
kind: cattle and creeping things and wild animals of the earth of
every kind.' And it was so.

God said, 'See, I have given you every plant yielding seed that is upon the face of all the earth, and every tree with seed in its fruit; you shall have them for food. And to every beast of the earth, and to every bird of the air, and to everything that creeps on the earth, everything that has the breath of life, I have given every green plant for food.' And it was so. God saw everything that he had made, and indeed, it was very good. (Gen. 1.1–2, 24, 29–31a)

Or (b):
The wolf shall live with the lamb,
the leopard shall lie down with the kid,
the calf and the lion and the fatling together,
and a little child shall lead them.
The cow and the bear shall graze,
their young shall lie down together;
and the lion shall eat straw like the ox.
The nursing child shall play over the hole of the asp,
and the weaned child shall put its hand on the adder's den.
They will not hurt or destroy
on all my holy mountain;
for the earth will be full of the knowledge of the LORD
as the waters cover the sea. (Isa. 11.6–9)

All praise be yours through Brother Wolf,
All praise be yours through Sister Whale,
By Nature's song my Lord be praised,
By Brother Eagle, Sister Loon.
Thru Sister Flower, Brother Tree.
Let Creatures all give thanks to thee.
All praise to those who live in peace.
(Scott Winter, based on St Francis of Assisi)

Second reading

Either (a):
I consider that the sufferings of this present time are not worth comparing with the glory about to be revealed to us. For the creation waits with eager longing for the revealing of the children of God; for the creation was subjected to futility, not of its own will but by the will of the one who subjected it, in hope that the creation itself will be set free from its bondage to decay and will obtain the freedom of the glory of the children of God. We know that the whole creation has been groaning in labour pains until now; and not only

the creation, but we ourselves, who have the first fruits of the Spirit, groan inwardly while we wait for adoption, the redemption of our bodies. (Rom. 8.18–23)

Or (b):
[St Francis] exulted in all the works of the Lord's hands, and looked beyond such pleasant sights to their life-giving cause and principle. In beautiful things he recognized God who is supremely beautiful; all good things cried out to him, 'He who made us is the best.'
He embraced all things with an unspoken rapture of devotion, speaking to them of the Lord and exhorting them to praise him.
When the brothers were cutting wood he forbade them to cut down a whole tree, so that it might have hope of sprouting again. He ordered the gardener not to dig up the border around the garden, in order that in season the greenness of grass and the beauty of flowers might proclaim the beauty of the Father of all things.
He picked up worms from the road that they might not be trodden on, and ordered honey and the best wine to be provided for bees that they might not perish from want in the cold of winter. He called all animals by the name of brother [or sister], though in all their kinds the gentle ones were his favourites. For that original goodness, which one day will be in each and every thing, already shone forth to this saint as in all things.[19]

Sermon

There follows an address or sermon on some aspect of Christian responsibility for the created world. A suggested text is 'The righteous care for their animals, but the wicked are cruel.' (Prov. 12.10)

Prayers

The following litany may be said:

Minister: Let us pray with the whole church and in the words of its saints, poets and theologians for all those who struggle against the abuse of animals and for the rebirth of compassion in our hearts:
Every creature is by its nature a kind of effigy and likeness of the eternal Wisdom. (St Bonaventure, 1221–74)

Reader: Almighty God, we pray for grace to perceive your creative hand in all things.

Minister: Lord in your mercy
Hear our prayer.

Minister: Surely we ought to show kindness and gentleness to animals for many reasons and chiefly because they are of the same origin as ourselves. (St John Chrysostom, *c.*347–407)

Reader: Increase in us, O God, a sense of fellowship with all your creatures. Help us to walk humbly and tread gently on your good earth.

Minister: Lord in your mercy
Hear our prayer.

Minister: What is a charitable heart? It is a heart which is burning with love for the whole creation ... a heart which can no longer bear to see or learn from others of any suffering, even the smallest pain, being inflicted on a creature. (St Isaac the Syrian, *c.*347–438)

Reader: Almighty God, we pray for loving sensitive hearts towards all your creatures.

Minister: Lord in your mercy
Hear our prayer.

Minister: A robin redbreast in a cage
Puts all heaven in a rage. (William Blake, 1757–1827)

Reader: Help us, O God, to set animals free from our own cruelty and greed.

Minister: Lord in your mercy
Hear our prayer.

Minister: I was early convinced in my mind that true religion consisted in an inward life, wherein the heart doth love and reverence God the Creator and learn to exercise true justice and goodness not only towards all [people] but also towards the [animal] creatures. (John Woolman, 1720–72)

Reader: Dear God, help us to recover humility in our relations with animals and to realize that it is the vocation of the strong to be gentle.

Minister: Lord in your mercy
Hear our prayer.

Minister: It must be remembered that we are required to practise justice even in our dealings with animals. (John Calvin, 1509–64)

Reader: Almighty God, help us to deal justly with animals, living
without wantonness and promoting kindness.

Minister: Lord in your mercy,
Hear our prayer.

Almighty God, we give thanks for all those who have gone
before us and given us examples of courage, mercy and faith.
Lord of all life,
your creation groans in travail
awaiting the glorious liberty
of the children of God;
by your Spirit help us
to free creation
from its bondage,
to heal its pain
and obtain that liberty
which is your gift to all creatures.
Amen.

Animals are now blessed in turn by the minister, who can move
between them in an outdoor setting

May God Almighty
Father, Son and Holy Spirit
bless this creature
protect it from cruelty
and grant it
a share in the redemption
of the world.
Amen.

One or more of the following prayers may be said:

Heavenly Father,
your Holy Spirit
gives breath to all living things;
renew us by the same Spirit
that we may learn to respect
what you have given
and care for what you have made,
through Jesus Christ
your Son, our Lord.
Amen.

Almighty God,
your Son, Jesus Christ,
taught us to love
even the least among us;
give us the courage to care
for all living creatures
and the strength to defend
even the weakest of all.
Amen.

Holy Father,
your Son Jesus Christ
is the reconciler of all things
in heaven and on earth;
send us your Spirit
that we may be made one
with all your creatures,
and know that all things
come from you,
and belong to you,
now and forever.
Amen.

The general blessing may now be given

Eternal Father, by your power of love you cause all things
to be, strengthen by the merciful example of your Son,
Jesus Christ, all those who struggle and work for the
alleviation of suffering, prosper their endeavours by the
power of your Holy Spirit; and may the blessing of God
Almighty, Creator, Redeemer and Sanctifier, be upon you
and remain with you always.
Amen.

Blessing of the Animals: A Short Service

Short and well-focused, this brief prayer service offers a touching sense of common purpose with our fellow creatures. It expresses in modern and poetic language the timeless spirituality of connection to creation, something that inspired the writer of the psalms in early Jewish history and continues to resonate today.

The service was put together by Nick Utphall, pastor of the Advent Lutheran Church/Madison Christian Community in Madison, Wisconsin. Nick is also director of the Let All Creation Praise website and resource centre, which offers a range of excellent outdoor and creation-orientated material.[20] It is reproduced with his kind permission. The liturgy is largely based on a version of Psalm 104 taken from *The Message* Bible translation.[21]

Blessing of the Animals: A Short Service

Welcome

The minister welcomes the gathering to this service

Opening Prayer

Minister: Good and loving Creator, we give you thanks for calling us into the circle of life, for the wonder of every creature, and for the joy, friendship, and love we share with our pets. Amen.

All: Amen.

Reading: Based on Psalm 104

Bless the LORD, O my soul, for God's good creation.
God, my God, how great you are!

You started the springs and rivers,
sent them flowing among the hills.
All the wild animals now drink their fill, wild donkeys
quench their thirst.
Along the riverbanks the birds build nests, ravens make
their voices heard.

Bless the LORD, O my soul, for God's good creation.
God, my God, how great you are!
Your trees are well-watered –
the Lebanon cedars you planted.
Birds build their nests in those trees;
Look – the stork at home in the treetop.
Mountain goats climb about the cliffs;
badgers burrow among the rocks.

Bless the LORD, O my soul, for God's good creation.
God, my God, how great you are!
When it's dark and night takes over,
all the forest creatures come out.
The young lions roar for their prey,
clamouring to you for their supper.
When the sun comes up, they vanish,
lazily stretched out in their dens.

Bless the LORD, O my soul, for God's good creation.
What a wildly wonderful world, God!
You made it all, with Wisdom at your side,
made earth overflow with your wonderful creations.
You even made the deep, wide sea,
brimming with fish past counting,
sardines and sharks and salmon.

Bless the LORD, O my soul, for God's good creation.

Prayer for the animals

O God, we pray for all the animals of the earth today:
Watch over our pets,
and those waiting to be adopted.
Watch over the wild animals,
and the habitats they call home.
Help us to be good stewards of the gifts of creation. Amen.

The Prayer of St Modestus for Animals

Outstanding for its great age as well as its powerful compassion for animals, this prayer arises from the cult of St Modestus, patriarch of Jerusalem in the seventh century. It is notable for its embrace of the goodness of all creation, and its concern to alleviate the suffering of animals out of sympathy for their 'bleating and noises' of distress. The prayer is preserved in the writings of St Nikodemos the Hagiorite, who compiled anthologies of many great early Christian texts on Mount Athos in the early nineteenth century. Since it refers to the saint's own relics it is safe to say it must have been written by one of his followers after his death.

A separate legend of St Modestus's life records that he once visited a widow in a dream and advised her to try a healing ritual to cure her oxen, using a home-made metal cross and some oil from her local church to anoint her animals in the field. Altogether, his witness stands as a remarkably powerful expression of the power of ritual to operate beyond the walls of a church building.

This prayer is reproduced with kind permission from the resources of the Pan-Orthodox Concern for Animals, a charity based in the UK which promotes Christian respect and responsibility for animals, with particular reference to Eastern Orthodox teachings and traditions. The charity's website is: panorthodoxconcernforanimals.org.

The prayer of St Modestus

Lord Jesus Christ my God, you who are merciful and all-good, who in wisdom created every visible and invisible creature, who pours out his compassions upon all that he created, who through your all-good providence foresees and troubles over all your creatures: bodiless, physical, rational, irrational, soul-bearing, soulless, from the first to the last. For nothing is not foreseen by you, neither is anything abandoned by you, the creator and foreseer of all.

For you are he who opens his hand and fills all living things with goodness. You are he who makes grass grow for the cattle, and green herbs for the service of humankind. You are he who once, through the herd of Israel, preserved them from above from the fatal wound of the first-born of the Egyptians.

You are he who, through the compassion of your Incarnation, deposed he who had the might of death: that is, the devil, and by your death, you put death to death. You are he who, through myself, your unworthy servant, puts to death the serpent, that your spring of water might not be corrupted. Those that drink from it, both the living and the dead, through your life-giving power, you resurrect. And if a demon draws near to it, and prepares to make itself apparent, seize it, that it might never dare to approach the place in which, I the sinner, call upon your name.

To you, therefore, I pray, O all-good master and creator of all, and I entreat you, the cause of all life, hearken to this my entreaty, and drive away every fatal sickness and danger from the oxen, horses, donkeys, mules, sheep, goats, bees and any other animals in true need to the life of your servants who call upon you, the giver of every good, and of my name.

And grant, O Lord, to all those who celebrate my name, and with faith hasten to the relics of St Modestus, permanent peace, multiplication of animals, uncorrupted wheat, wine and oil, and above all, remission of sins, health of bodies, and eternal salvation of souls. Yes, O Lord Jesus Christ, for the descendants from your very loins, grant compassion on the suffering animals, whose herd is being afflicted by the sickle of death. And having no word besides bleating and bitter and random noises, in your mercy take away their passion and suffering. For if you even call rational beings to this sympathy – 'A righteous man has compassion upon his animals,' as is written – how much more do you show compassion on these, who are their creator and foreseer?

For you, O compassionate one, preserved the animals in the Ark, as your goodness and compassions won out. That by the wellness and multiplication of the oxen, and the remaining four-legged animals, the earth might be worked, and fruit might be harvested, and your servants who call upon my name might be preserved without any corruption and partake of their very harvest. And that these, having all things that are necessary, might be increased in every good work, and glorify you, who grants every good thing. And grant me also, your servant and most-fervent supplicant, the honour of your all-governing kingdom, for to you belong all glory, honour and worship, with your beginning-less Father, and your all-holy and good and life-giving Spirit, now and ever, and unto the ages of ages.
Amen.

Blessing for Animal Welfare Staff and Sanctuaries

Blessings for buildings and specific places are commonplace in Christian tradition, and this short formula extends the church's ministry of care to encompass the work of animal welfare shelters and homes, and their resident creatures. The blessing was created at the instigation of Dr Christina Nellist of the Pan-Orthodox Concern for Animals charity. The blessing was composed by Fr Simon Peter Nellist, Archpriest of Tanzania, by combining traditional Orthodox intercessions with prayers composed by Professor Andrew Linzey, whose animal services appear on pages 19 and 24.

The blessing is reproduced with kind permission from both the charity and Professor Linzey. For more information on their work see panorthodoxconcernforanimals.org and www.oxfordanimalethics.com.

A blessing for animal welfare staff and sanctuaries

Blessed is our God, always now and forever and to the ages of ages. Amen.
In the beginning God created the heavens and the earth and God saw that everything he made was very good.

Almighty God, we come together to thank you for the beauty and glory of your creation; to acknowledge our responsibility to animals and for our use of the created world.

Let us pray with the whole church for all those who struggle against the abuse of animals and for the strengthening of compassion in our hearts. Give those who work in this sanctuary the strength to continue to rescue and care for your creatures abused by others. We also pray for the animals in this shelter who were abandoned and abused; neglected and ill-treated.

Holy God, your mercies are all over the earth, bless the creatures in this sanctuary and those that care for them and help us delight in the works of your hands.

Blessed before you, O God, are those who struggle for peace and harmony in your creation. Strengthen their endeavours by the power of your Holy Spirit and may the blessing of God almighty, Father, Son and Holy Spirit, be upon them.

O Creator and author of all things, giver of all spiritual graces and bestower of eternal salvation, send down your Holy Spirit with a blessing from upon high for this animal sanctuary that, fortified by the might of your heavenly protection, it may fulfil its promises to the animals of [*name of the local town or community*] and all who make use of it.

Through Jesus Christ our Lord, we in turn, send you our praises and love, both now and forever and to the ages of ages. Amen.

Prayer at the Death of Companion Animals

The powerful human need to mark and grieve for the death of a companion animal is given thoughtful expression in this short and meaningful prayer, a synthesis of ancient and modern writings. It was composed by Fr Simon Peter Nellist, Archpriest of Tanzania, based on prayers by Professor Andrew Linzey and incorporating some traditional Orthodox prayers.

It is reproduced with kind permission from both the Pan-Orthodox Concern for Animals charity and Professor Linzey. For more information on their work see panorthodoxconcernforanimals.org and www. oxfordanimalethics.com.

Prayer at the death of companion animals

Holy God, Holy Mighty, Holy Immortal, have mercy on us. (*said three times*)
Glory to the Father and to the Son and to the Holy Spirit, now and ever and to the ages of ages. Amen.

Holy God, everything that has breath praises you both in this world and the next. In your all-encompassing mercy, O God, we now commit the life of this our beloved friend and companion [*name*] to eternal fellowship with you.

Create within us a spirit of gratitude for the life of [*name*]. Give rest, O God, to [*name*] who lived among us and gave us freely of [his/her] love.

Holy Father, your son Jesus Christ taught us that not one sparrow is forgotten in your sight; we ask therefore for you to provide a place of green pasture where [his/her] praises will be heard in your presence and where [he/she] shall be free from suffering and pain.

God our Creator, hear our prayer:
Glory to you, O Christ our God, the origin and destiny of all
    living things;
Glory to you, O Christ our God, who bears the wounds of all
    suffering;
Glory to you, O Christ our God, who transforms suffering into joy.
You are the God who creates and the God who reconciles and
    redeems all creation.
Glory to you, O Christ our God and saviour of the universe: in Christ
    shall all be made alive.
Holy God, holy mighty, holy immortal, have mercy on us.
    (*said three times*)
Glory to the Father and to the Son and to the Holy Spirit, now and
    ever and to the ages of ages. Amen.

LOVE FEASTS AND
COMMUNITY GATHERINGS

'Table fellowship' has a long and noble place in church tradition, an idea which has on occasion prompted Christians to move outdoors to enjoy shared meals in the fresh air. As a model for a church picnic – a communal meal with an element of ritual and spiritual significance – the following patterns of worship seem just as suitable today as they have done throughout Christian history.

The idea of Christians gathering for a celebratory meal appears remarkably early in church history, described by St Paul in 1 Corinthians 11.17–34. It is clearly the setting in which the Eucharist was celebrated, a distinct ritual at the end of this communal meal. Such a gathering was (and is) called a 'love-feast' or an *agape*-feast, *agape* being the Greek word for the highest form of charitable, self-giving love. This very word appears in plural form in the New Testament to describe the meals shared by the early church in Jude 1.12 and 2 Peter 2.13.

If the term 'love-feast' seems to hint at something other than a devout gathering for purely spiritual purposes, it might be consolation to know that the early church suffered just the same problem. Paul's own letter to the Corinthians goes on at some length about the tendency for love-feast gatherings to degenerate into parties marked by gluttony and drunkenness, while the references in Jude and 2 Peter also refer to those coming along purely to overindulge. Perhaps it is unsurprising that the church abandoned the whole practice by the fourth century, a forgotten Christian tradition that was only revived as late as the eighteenth century by reformers including John Wesley, founder of the Methodist Church. The Methodist Church in America picked up the idea of the love-feast and made them part of its camp meetings, which were held in the outdoors. The collection of liturgies offered below includes a modern reinvention of this tradition that was established in Sausalito, California.

Attempts to start camp meetings in Britain, inspired by the American example, took place at a village called Mow Cop in Cheshire. As one of the organizers put it: 'Worship in the open air commenced with Adam and Eve in the Garden of Eden, when in a state of innocence ... Our Lord Jesus Christ carried on religious services in the open air, and his apostles followed the example.'[22] Alas, such al fresco spirituality was met with disapproval by the Methodist hierarchy, and in part led to the formation of the breakaway Society of Primitive Methodists.

Today a love-feast offers an authentic opportunity to gather for an outdoor meal such as a picnic and share food together in a meaningful way. It is particularly helpful as a model for an ecumenical gathering, the shared meal being reminiscent of a Eucharist but without the need for any one church tradition to preside over the formal sacraments using bread and wine. In the Methodist tradition, it is interesting to note that recipes from the time of John Wesley can still be found today for baking an authentic love-feast cake, as described below.

A traditional love-feast cake recipe

This recipe is adapted from the Middlesmoor Lovefeast Bread used in the Yorkshire Dales at the time of John Wesley.[23]

- 1lb (400g) plain flour
- 1oz (25g) baking powder
- 5oz (125g) butter
- 8oz (200g) sugar
- 4oz (100g) sultanas
- 2oz (50g) mixed peel
- 2 eggs
- About half a pint (280ml) of milk

Mix the flour and baking powder together, rub in the butter, then add the sugar, sultanas and peel.

Beat the eggs together with a little milk and add to the dry ingredients.

Add the rest of the milk to make a soft consistency.

Pour the mixture into two loaf tins or a large cake tin.

Cook at 180°C (350°F) or gas mark 4 for at least 45 minutes for the loaf tins, or 1 hour for the large cake tin.

Love-feast grace

This early form of grace was developed for the love-feast by John Cennick, one of the early Methodist preachers, and is recorded in his book of hymns.[24] Its reference to creatures and to paradise resonate particularly well with an outdoor setting.

Minister: Be present at our table, Lord;
            Be here and everywhere adored;
            Thy creatures bless, and grant that we
            May feast in paradise with thee.
All: **Amen.**

Liturgy for a Love-Feast: A Time of Centring

This liturgy was composed by Dr Cynthia A. Wilson, executive director of Worship Resources in the Discipleship Ministries Agency of the United Methodist Church, based in Nashville, Tennessee. It is a Wesleyan love-feast, a modern adaptation of a liturgy that pays full homage to both the original Methodist service and older traditions still. It includes a prayer from the important first-century Christian document known as the *Didache*. It is reproduced here with the kind permission of Cynthia.[25]

Liturgy for a Love-Feast

Greeting

Brothers and sisters in Christ, we have all come to this place frail and broken. In a world of violence, hate, greed and isolation, in a church searching to find the way forward, we look for healing through this restorative service of old. It is in this *agape*-feast where adversaries become friends, friends become neighbours, and the Christian family embraces all. Let us join in song before we share the blessings of food and water, just as the first Christians did in ancient times.

The history of the feast, as a celebration born simply out of love, generosity and fellowship, is beautiful. Christians today must be grateful for the resurrection of the celebration by the Moravians, and also for the vitality given to it by Charles Wesley! The feast is appropriate in any Christian setting and can nourish the hearts and souls of Christians in so many ways. At its most basic, the love-feast is an experience of warmth and sharing, a commemoration of the early church. At its most symbolic, the love-feast is a means of God's grace that is experienced in the fellowship with each other and with God. But the simplest explanation of the love-feast, to which one can respond when asked, is that it is a way to remember Christ's presence on earth, and to celebrate with gratitude the spirit of God's love.

Opening Hymn

'What feast of love'[26]

Opening prayer (based on the *Didache*, early Christian text)

We thank you, O God, for the life and knowledge which you have revealed through Jesus, your child and our brother. To you be glory forever.
As the piece of bread was scattered over the hills and then brought together and made one, so, let your church be brought together from the ends of the earth into your kingdom.
For yours is the glory and the power through Jesus Christ forever. Amen.

Scripture readings

Galatians 3.26–29: Baptized into Christ
For in Christ Jesus you are all children of God through faith. As many of you as were baptized into Christ have clothed yourselves with Christ. There is no longer Jew or Greek, there is no longer slave or free, there is no longer male and female; for all of you are one in Christ Jesus. And if you belong to Christ, then you are Abraham's offspring, heirs according to the promise.

Ephesians 4.1–6: Unity in the body of Christ
I, therefore, the prisoner in the Lord, beg you to lead a life worthy of the calling to which you have been called, with all humility and gentleness, with patience, bearing with one another in love, making every effort to maintain the unity of the Spirit in the bond of peace. There is one body and one Spirit, just as you were called to the one hope of your calling, one Lord, one faith, one baptism, one God and Father of all, who is above all and through all and in all.

Meditation

Hymn

'We are one in the Spirit'[27]

The Agape Feast

Here before us, you will find some water and bread. It is important to know that this feast is not a Eucharistic feast, but one of love and fellowship.
Let us commemorate our unity through Christ, and feast on the spirit of love who is Christ.

Here the agape loaf or cake (see page 40 for an authentic recipe) is shared, and water distributed

The blessing

Hymn

Suggested hymn: Song of sending – 'Zion still sings' *from* Methodist Worship Book #219

Liturgy for a Love-Feast: Katrina's Dream

This liturgy was written by Helene de Boissiere-Swanson as part of a programme of activity by Katrina's Dream, a charitable organization based in Washington, DC, in the US.[28] The charity was set up in memory of Revd Katrina Swanson, the first woman priest in the American Episcopal church to have a parish, and campaigns for the full inclusion of women in church life and in wider society. Katrina Swanson had a ministry  to travellers and homeless people, and even stipulated that a public bench dedicated to her should be designed so it could be used by rough sleepers. It was considered entirely fitting that an outdoor love-feast or *agape* be held in her honour, for which the following liturgy was crafted by Helene and conducted by her husband William Swanson at a service held in Dunphy Park, Sausalito, near San Francisco in 2011. It was aimed in particular at impoverished sailors and seafarers.

Liturgy for a Love-Feast

Introduction

Leader: *Agape* is the New Testament Greek word for self-giving love. In the Christian tradition an *agape* is also the name for informal meals and times of togetherness and mutual sharing, which remind us of all those early Christians' love-feasts and the unity that the Spirit continues to give us.

A bell is rung

The blessing of the meal

Leader: How wonderful it is, how pleasant, for God's people to live together in harmony! Welcome to this meal, in the name of Christ. We come to share in God's love.

All: **We come to share our food and our lives.**

We come to break bread together, and open ourselves to each other.
We come to express our faith and our thanks.

May God bless this food and this fellowship.
As we share our food, we give thanks for this abundance, and we remember those who do not have enough.

May God give food to those who are hungry.
May God give us a hunger for justice, and a determination to serve those who hunger for food.

Setting the table

On the table in the midst of this community with whom Christ is present we set symbols to remind us of his promises to us:

Reader 1: A candle, to remind us of the way, 'I am the light of the world; whoever follows me will not walk in darkness but will have the light of life.'

Reader 2: Bread, a symbol to remind us of God's love, 'I am the bread of life. The bread that I shall give is myself for the life of the world.'
God, we welcome your presence with us. May the food and companionship we share nourish our bodies, hearts and minds. And may our spirits be refreshed. As we live in the light of your presence. With us now, and at all times and places. Amen.

Food is served. People share stories when the meal is finished.

The peace

Leader: Behold, the fragments of our feast. Our meal is ended, but God's banquet continues as we go from this place.
Let us take the banquet into the world and never give up until all people are fed.

May the peace of Christ be upon you, and may you be channels of peace and justice.
Amen.

A closing song or hymn is sung; one suggested choice is 'They will know we are Christians by our love', by Peter Sholtes

Liturgy for a Love-Feast: UK Methodist Version

As far as written evidence suggests, the first love-feasts celebrated by the early Methodists did not follow a rigid pattern, and were not considered formal liturgy as such. But they did include a number of common elements, which have been assembled together for this suggested structure to help shape a modern gathering. For a detailed introduction to the early love-feasts, David M. Chapman's study of the origins of Methodism has a chapter devoted to their development, which explains their place in outdoor worship.[29] Accordingly it can be suggested that a traditional love-feast gathering included the following elements, although not necessarily in this order:

Liturgy for a Love-Feast

Hymn
Prayer
Grace
Distribution of bread or cake
Collection for the poor
Circulation of a shared cup (the 'loving cup')
Address by the minister
Testimonies prepared by members of the gathering
Open time of prayer and praise
Closing words from the minister
Hymn
Blessing

With this structure in mind, the Methodist Church in the UK has produced a modern love-feast liturgy, paying close attention to the details of the traditional gathering.

Notes on preparation

Love-feasts often follow a fairly simple supper, lunch or tea-time meal at which regular conversation has taken place. The love-feast, in common with other acts of worship, includes prayer, praise, scripture, preaching and mutual fellowship and an offering. It also offers a time for prepared testimony and of course the sharing of the love-feast cake and the loving cup. The plate of love-feast cake (each portion about 2 or 3 cm square) and the loving cup (or jug of water, if individual glasses or cups are to be used) are covered until they are required, and are placed near the one leading the celebration (who may be lay or ordained). A traditional recipe for a love feast cake dating from the time of John Wesley is reproduced on page 40.

Introduction

Minister: The love-feast, or *agape*, is a Christian fellowship meal recalling the meals Jesus shared with disciples during his ministry. This service expresses *koinonia* or sharing: the belonging and fellowship enjoyed within the body of Christ.

A suggested order for a love-feast

1 A hymn such as 'All praise to our redeeming Lord' (*Singing the Faith* 608) or 'Jesus, lover of my soul' (*Singing the Faith* 355) or a range of worship songs.
2 A prayer rejoicing in God's presence and the gift of salvation in Christ and seeking the blessing of the Holy Spirit.
3 Previously prepared testimony is shared.
4 A Bible reading such as: Isaiah 55.1–3; Isaiah 55.6–11; Romans 5.1–5; 1 Corinthians 13; Ephesians 3.14–19; Philippians 2.1–11; 1 John 4.7–21; Matthew 22.34–40; Revelation 19.6–9.
5 A short sermon may be preached.
6 A hymn is sung, such as Charles Wesley's 'Come, and let us sweetly join', and during the singing a collection is made for those in need. Charles Wesley wrote this hymn specifically for love-feast gatherings, with 22 eight-line verses in the original.[30] Some verses from this hymn appear in *Singing the Faith* 646, and a shorter version is printed here.

Come, and let us sweetly join
Christ to praise in hymns divine;
Give we all with one accord
Glory to our common Lord.

Hands and hearts and voices raise,
Sing as in the ancient days,
Antedate the joys above,
Celebrate the feast of love.

Jesu, dear expected Guest,
Thou art bidden to the feast;
For thyself our hearts prepare,
Come, and rest, and banquet there.

Sanctify us, Lord, and bless,
Breathe thy Spirit, give thy peace;
Thou thyself within us move,
Make our feast a feast of love.

7   The plate with portions of love-feast cake is circulated. Each person receives and retains their portion as participants pass the plate to their neighbour.

8   The singing of a love-feast grace, such as the following:

> Be present at our table, Lord;
> be here and everywhere adored;
> thy creatures bless, and grant that we
> may feast in paradise with thee.

This may be sung to any Long Metre tune, such as Rimington (Singing the Faith 328ii) *or Old Hundredth* (Singing the Faith 1).

9   The portions of love-feast cake are eaten in silence.

10 The loving cup is then passed in silence (or each person's glass is filled from the jug) and each person takes a sip of the water.

11 Responses to God's grace and goodness are then invited. This could include sharing reflections on the testimony offered, the scriptures read and the sermon. This could also include practical responses to the needs of the world through charitable giving or making commitments to particular social action.

12 Prayers of thanksgiving and intercession are offered in a prepared, extempore or spontaneous form.

13 A hymn such as 'Christ, from whom all blessings flow' (*Singing the Faith* 676).

14 A benediction or blessing.

3

CHURCHYARD, PARISH AND ROGATION BLESSING RITUALS

The Rogation procession around a parish is one of the most obvious examples of an outdoor church ritual still in common use today. Certainly in Britain the practice of walking round the boundary of a parish during Rogationtide, the three days before Ascension day, is well known and many national church bodies offer formal liturgies to help structure the event. This chapter can therefore be considered a supplement of additional resources to use for such processions, but with one important dimension: processions into and around the vicinity of a church have many origins and purposes beyond simply following a parish boundary. To that end it is suggested that a church procession could be considered in a new light, and undertaken as a form of 'parish pilgrimage': a walk that pays respects to a number of spiritually significant places around the local community. This also happens to be closer to the original form of the Rogation procession.

The Rogation service as we understand it today has reached us through a number of twists and liturgical innovations over the centuries. It has a long pedigree, with roots in the late fifth century, and it is worth spending some time unravelling the threads that have been woven together into the current modern expressions of very old traditions. For they serve a number of separate if complementary functions: prayers for a community's safety and success, an act of public repentance, a circuitous walk to mark out a parish or similar boundary, processions between spiritually significant sites within a local area and agricultural prayers over newly planted fields, among others.

The Rogation procession was first introduced by St Mamertus, bishop of Vienne in south-west France, who died around AD 475. The saint was reacting to the threat of fires, earthquakes and unexplained sounds in the night; a list of woes that illustrates a period of upheaval and dismay. All of that certainly applies to fifth-century Europe, as communities lamented the collapse of the powerful Roman Empire and the accompanying threat of wars, famines and civil unrest. Immediately after a huge fire had threatened the city, and was only extinguished following his prayers, Mamertus decided to institute the Rogation service as a means of expressing communal grief, repentance and solidarity.

There are early writers who mention these prototype Rogation processions, which quickly caught the imagination of both the people of Vienne and the wider church. Mamertus was initially hesitant to introduce the ceremony, picking an inconspicuous church in the city from which to attempt the first procession, and was pleasantly surprised by its popular uptake.[31]

All early descriptions of Mamertus' innovative service depict a procession marked by remorse and repentance, the prayers embellished with the tears of the faithful. It was not long before these Rogation processions became an enduring feature of church life across Europe, and remain so to this day. They were mandated in Anglo-Saxon England at the Council of Clovesho in AD 747, and were no doubt performed before then too.

This and other evidence indicates that such early processions were not originally intended to mark out the boundary of a parish, at least not in the sense that we currently map out its geographical limits, a feature known as 'beating the bounds'. Rather they were processions around a different sort of boundary, a 'spiritual boundary' one might say, visiting sites of sacred power in the landscape that had undergone some sort of assimilation into Christian tradition. Holy wells and sacred trees, along with occasional landmark boulders, would be good examples of this. A procession today could easily justify visiting local parish sights such as a landmark tree to read the Bible passages, an ancient tradition that bequeathed us the notion of the Gospel Oak in the UK. Crosses and monuments in the landscape have also been visited by Rogation processions from Anglo-Saxon times onwards, and a market cross or a war memorial would serve the purpose well today.[32]

A modern parish procession could therefore be revived not in the proprietorial sense of delimiting the land of any particular parish by walking along its boundaries, but by procession to sites of particular spiritual or community significance. This could work in any parish, whether urban or rural, from a landmark tree in a park at one end of the scale to a hilltop summit at the other. 'Beating the bounds' does not therefore necessarily need to be a territorial rite, but rather a way of touching spiritual boundaries instead, interacting with the interface between humans and the natural world.

This coalesces neatly with a theology of 'thin places', the phrase used in Celtic Christian circles to describe sites where heaven seems particularly close on earth, where the boundary between the spiritual realm is thin. A tree, river, park, garden or even small, inner-city churchyard can embody such an instinct in even the most urban of settings. Some of the following liturgies suggest that woven crosses can be blessed in church and then taken and buried or planted at a field or garden edge, an ancient tradition recorded in the Anglo-Saxon Æcerbot ritual. A Brigid's Cross, woven from rushes or reeds, would be a particularly suitable and resonant tradition to revive for this.

A procession around the whole parish boundary is therefore only a small part of the landscape liturgies covered in this chapter. A procession around the churchyard itself, a local park or a farm would be just as meaningful, as are the other prayers of blessing for various forms of communal outdoor space.

Clipping Service

A clipping service is one of those community rituals so ancient its origins are lost in the mists of time. Such a gap in our knowledge invariably attracts speculation as to possible pagan antecedents, although the current form of the liturgy could not be more ecclesiastical in character: once a year the congregation file out of church during the special clipping service and link hands in a very large circle to encompass the building. Prayers are directed towards both the church and its surrounding community.

The word 'clipping' derives from the medieval word *yclept*, which means 'to embrace'. The practice ceased after the Reformation, one of many folk expressions of piety that fell foul of new restrictions on popular religious culture, only to be revived again in Victorian times.

This ritual could be repurposed for use by any Christian establishment, such as a church school, as an inventive way to capture the imagination of younger members of the community. Clipping is usually performed on Shrove Tuesday, Mothering Sunday, Easter Monday, or on a church's patronal festival.

The service reproduced here is from the parish church of St Andrew's Church Wissett, of the Blyth Valley Team Ministry in north-east Suffolk, and takes place on Shrove Tuesday. The occasion is ecumenical, and a Salvation Army band accompanies the singing of 'Lord of the Dance'. Variations of the clipping service performed today at other churches involve a chain dance around the churchyard, including a 'threading the needle' where the leading couple make an arch with their arms for the line of dancers to go under.

St Andrew's has been celebrating clipping since 1995. As at other churches, the service begins indoors before the congregation processes outside to complete the clipping. Towards the end of the service the congregation gathers by a statue of St Andrew to say a prayer about their patron, a reminder that so many liturgies in this book can, and do, take on a local theme. The text is reproduced by kind permission of the vicar and churchwardens of St Andrew's Church Wissett.

The clipping service

Minister: How awesome is this place!
All: **This is none other than the house of God.**
           This is the gate of heaven.

Hymn

Almighty God, in your love you have given us this house of prayer:
we praise you for the many blessings you have given to those who
worship you here:
and we pray that all who seek you in this place may find you,
and, being filled with the Holy Spirit, may become a living temple
acceptable to you;
through Jesus Christ your Son our Lord, who is alive and reigns with
you, in the unity of the Holy Spirit, one God, now and for ever.
Amen.

Please sit

Poems and readings

Hymn

The address

Hymn

Suggested hymn is 'Lord of the dance'

The procession and clipping

*The congregation process from the church and gather outside to
link hands, forming a human chain around the building. When the
clipping is complete all sing:*

Praise God from whom all blessings flow,
Praise him all creatures here below.
Praise him above, angelic host,
Praise Father, Son and Holy Ghost. Amen.

*At this point the congregation return to their pews, although the
service could continue outside once all are gathered*

The prayers

For the Church universal, of which this building is a visible symbol:
Lord, receive our thanks and prayer.

For this congregation, as we remember your promise that when two
or three are gathered in your name you are there in the midst of
them:
Lord, receive our thanks and prayer.

For this church, where we may be still and know that you are God:
Lord, receive our thanks and prayer.

For [*this village/town*], a place of companionship and community in
which your love dwells:
Lord, receive our thanks and prayer.

For the fulfilling of our desires and petitions as you see best for us:
Lord, receive our thanks and prayer.

For the faith of those who have gone before us and for grace to
persevere like them:
Lord, receive our thanks and prayer.

For all the benefactors of this place who have died in the peace of
Christ and are at rest:
Lord, receive our thanks and prayer.

For a sense of our fellowship with [*patron saint*] under whose
protection this church stands, and with all your saints:
Lord, receive our thanks and prayer.

O God, from living and chosen stones
you prepare an everlasting dwelling place for your majesty.
Grant that in the power of the Holy Spirit
those who serve you here on earth
may in the fullness of time sing your praise in heaven;
through Jesus Christ our Lord.
Amen.

How awesome is this place!
This is none other than the house of God.
This is the gate of heaven.

I saw a ladder which rested on the ground
with its top reaching to heaven
and the angels of God were going up and down it.

This is none other than the house of God.
This is the gate of heaven.

God our Father, in this house of prayer you bless your people on
their earthly pilgrimage.
Quicken our consciences by your holiness, nourish our minds by your
truth, purify our imaginations by your beauty, and open our hearts
to your love, that, in the surrender of our wills to your purpose, the
world may be renewed in Jesus Christ our Lord.
Amen.

Almighty God, give us who are called by your holy word grace to
follow without delay and to tell the good news of your kingdom;
through Jesus Christ our Lord.
Amen.

Hymn

The blessing

Go forth into the world in peace;
be of good courage:
hold fast to what is good;
render to no one evil for evil;
strengthen the fainthearted; support the weak;
help the afflicted; honour everyone;
love and serve the Lord,
rejoicing in the power of the Holy Spirit,
and the blessing + of God almighty,
the Father, the Son, and the Holy Spirit,
be among you and remain with you always.
Amen

Two Blessings of Green Things:
Crops, Grass and Herbs

Anglo-Saxon farmers and gardeners must have endured a fair share of suffering as they tilled the land, if these short but powerful blessing prayers are anything to go by. They both begin with a prayer over all manner of plants and move swiftly on to praying for the ailments of those who work the soil, blessing their produce as health-giving and restorative. The second prayer is a particularly important and rare piece of Christian landscape lore that merits revival, since it was composed for use in the middle of the growing season, referring to the festival of John the Baptist, 24 June. With Rogation marking the start of the growing season, and Lammas day at its end with the first harvest, this little prayer is a reminder that work continues between the activities of sowing and reaping.

It becomes easier to understand when using these prayers how far the early Christians merged together the ideas of spiritual and physical well-being, a reminder that the modern terms 'holy' and 'healthy' actually derive from a single Anglo-Saxon root term *hǣlu*, which is perhaps best encapsulated by the modern English word 'wholesome'. Good for body and soul alike, these two prayers therefore greatly commend themselves to anyone tending to plants or crops. They are recorded in a manuscript known as the *Hyde Register*, an eleventh-century text written and kept at Hyde Abbey in Winchester.[33]

A Blessing of Green Things

Almighty and eternal God, Creator and ruler of all your creatures who, by your Word and creating from nothing, did on the third day bid to come forth green living things and fruit bearing trees, to the perfection of your work. You ordered these living blooms of greenery for the health of the faithful, and whenever they are gathered, through the invocation of your most holy name, to bless and to sanctify by your customary piety, to deign and grant us, even with unworthy prayers, that anyone who labours with illness may overcome them all, preventing death by your mercy. May their languor vanish, the heat of fever diffuse, the pain inside and out depart and the striking infection of the enemy be sent away by you who with your co-eternal son and the Holy Spirit live and reign, one God through all ages for ever. Amen.

Another Blessing of Green Things

Lord Jesus Christ, Son of God, who from the majesty of the paternal bosom descended to us and deigned to offer all who believe in you healing salvation for our pollution and scars, proclaimed 'whatever you ask the Father in my name it will be done for you'. Be with us now as we seek you in our faith and by the intervening merit and intercessions of your mother Mary, ever-virgin, with all the saints and equally by the intervention of your Forerunner [John the Baptist] who is celebrated today on this day of his birth.

Bless and sanctify these blooms of green, which you have nourished to grow by fair weather and the abundance of dew that, by the invocation of your most holy name, they may be to whoever is labouring in infirmity a cure and remedy, wiping away languor, and a remedy to soul and body through you, Jesus Christ who with the Father in the unity of the Holy Spirit is glorified, God through all eternity. Amen.

The Blessing of Public Utilities: Roman Catholic Order

Important but all too often overlooked, public utilities and other technical installations can be placed at the centre of a community's prayers and thanksgiving with this service produced by the Roman Catholic Church. All manner of public amenities and processing centres help to manage the environment, from waste processing plants, recycling centres and facilities, sewage and water treatment plants and reservoirs, and power generation facilities.

There are specific blessings designed for both processing plants and a reservoir or water system. The church stresses that this is a service for communal facilities, which means that it should include members of the team working at the site as well as the local community which benefits from it. The service is reproduced by kind permission of the International Commission on English in the Liturgy, and can also be found in the *Book of Blessings*, which also has a longer version of the blessing.[34]

Order for the Blessing of Technical Installations or Equipment

An introductory song or hymn can be sung

Minister: Let us give praise to God, who has set us over the works of his hands. Blessed be God now and for ever.

All: Amen.

Through the work of our hands and the help of technology we cooperate with the Creator to improve the earth as the dwelling place of the human family. By our efforts to bring the work of creation to perfection, we contribute to the advancement of society and carry out Christ's mandate to follow him in serving one another in love. Let us, then, bless God as we use these products of technology for our advantage and never forget to offer praise to him, who is the true light and the fount of that water which springs up to eternal life.

Reading

Reader: Brothers and sisters, listen to the words of the book of Genesis (Gen. 1.1–5a, 14–18):

God said: Let there be light, and there was light.

In the beginning when God created the heavens and the earth, the earth was a formless void and darkness covered the face of the deep, while a wind from God swept over the face of the waters. Then God said, 'Let there be light'; and there was light. And God saw that the light was good; and God separated the light from the darkness. God called the light Day, and the darkness he called Night.

And God said, 'Let there be lights in the dome of the sky to separate the day from the night; and let them be for signs and for seasons and for days and years, and let them be lights in the dome of the sky to give light upon the earth.' And it was so. God made the two great lights – the greater light to rule the day and the lesser light to rule the night – and the stars. God set them in the dome of the sky to give light upon the earth, to rule over the day and over the night, and to separate the light from the darkness. And God saw that it was good.

Psalm 18

Minister: The response to the psalm is: 'My God, you are always there to help me; I place my trust in you.'
My God, you are always there to help me; I place my trust in you.

He made darkness his covering around him,
his canopy thick clouds dark with water.
Out of the brightness before him
there broke through his clouds hailstones and coals of fire.
My God, you are always there to help me; I place my trust in you.

The LORD also thundered in the heavens,
and the Most High uttered his voice.
And he sent out his arrows, and scattered them;
he flashed forth lightnings, and routed them.
My God, you are always there to help me; I place my trust in you.

Then the channels of the sea were seen,
and the foundations of the world were laid bare
at your rebuke, O LORD,
at the blast of the breath of your nostrils.
**My God, you are always there to help me; I place my trust
in you.**

He reached down from on high, he took me;
he drew me out of mighty waters.
He brought me out into a broad place;
he delivered me, because he delighted in me.
**My God, you are always there to help me; I place my trust
in you.**

Intercessions

In human works and the inventions of human genius we
must recognize the continuing activity of God the Creator.
Rightly, then, we offer praise to God with grateful hearts
and call on him with confidence, saying:
Lord, sustain the work of our hands.

Assisting Eternal God, you made all things good and gave them into
Minister: our care; grant that we may use the forces of nature wisely
for your glory and our own well-being. For this we pray:
Lord, sustain the work of our hands.

You continually give us your Holy Spirit; grant that we
may cooperate with the same Spirit for the renewal of
the face of the earth, not merely through technology but
through justice and charity. For this we pray:
Lord, sustain the work of our hands.

You know what lies in our hearts; grant that a desire
for what is right and good will guide the use of scientific
knowledge. For this we pray:
Lord, sustain the work of our hands.

Your wish is that all should call you Father: grant that
those people who suffer discrimination may be helped by
all of us to gain the rights and advantages that belong to
every human being. For this we pray:
Lord, sustain the work of our hands.

Prayers of blessing

A Blessing of any kind of technical equipment

Blessed are you, Lord our God, and worthy of all praise, for you have provided for the perfecting of your creation through human labour and intelligence, and you show your own power and goodness in the inventions of the human race. Grant that all those who will use this equipment to improve their lives may recognize that you are wonderful in your works and may learn to carry out your will more readily.
We ask this through Christ our Lord.
Amen.

B Blessing of a central energy source or power house

Lord God, all-powerful Creator of light, Source and origin of us all, look with kindness upon your servants who will use this equipment to produce [electricity, atomic power]. Grant that by continuing to seek your face they may, after the darkness of this world, find you, the unfailing light, in whom we live and move and have our being.
We ask this through Christ our Lord.
Amen.

C Blessing of a reservoir or water system

Blessed are you, Lord our God, and worthy of all praise, for you have provided for the perfecting of your creation through human labour and intelligence, and you show your own power and goodness in the inventions of the human race.
Grant that all those who will use this supply of water for their needs may recognize that you are their living fountain, the source of the water that springs up to eternal life. We ask this through Christ our Lord.
Amen.

Concluding rite

After the prayer of blessing the equipment can be turned on for the first time, if it is a new facility

Minister: May God, from whom every good gift comes, make his countenance to shine upon us and guide us into the way of peace, now and for ever.
Amen.

A concluding hymn can be sung

A Traditional Rogation Liturgy

Many are the ways in which a Rogation procession can be conducted. This sequence of prayers, blessings and practices has been compiled by a team of Anglican priests based on a range of traditions in the Church of England. It offers a thoughtful recognition of the gifts of the natural world, reflecting the fact that Rogation processions take place during the season of planting, in northern hemisphere countries at least.

It comes in two parts, first a number of suggestions for ritual actions and prayers during a Eucharist in the church before the procession begins, and then a number of elements that can be included on the walk. As a means of breaking down the demarcation between ritual life inside the church and the wider world outside, therefore, it has much to commend it. The liturgy suggests that small crosses can be brought in to the church and blessed during the service before the procession begins, and the crosses later taken away and placed in fields and gardens. This echoes much older Rogation traditions, most notably in the *Æcerbot* ritual described on page 175. The crosses can be prepared by children, made with twigs or woven from grass, avoiding the use of any plastic twine or cable. A Brigid's Cross would be a pleasingly Celtic model for this, made from reeds or rushes to a pattern easily available online.

This configuration of the Rogation ritual makes the helpful suggestion that the procession can be conducted between important points within the parish, an alternative to the idea of a circumambulation around the parish boundary as described in the introduction to this chapter. If such a 'parish pilgrimage' appeals, the formula below includes prayers at a range of significant places. It also includes the famous prayer attributed to St Francis calling for reconciliation, a reminder of the role of good neighbourly relationships wherever a boundary feature is included in the procession.

A Rogation ritual can also involve processing with a number of items, including the processional cross at the front, torches, a church banner, incense, holy water, an icon, personal crosses and other symbols. It is traditional to sing litanies, psalms and hymns while walking, including the Great Litany contained in the Book of Common Prayer. All told, this liturgy contains a number of meaningful ritual elements which are described in further detail on the website of Full Homely Divinity,[35] which has kindly given permission for this compilation to be published here.

Rogation Liturgy

Preparatory note for a Rogation Eucharist service

The Offertory element of a Eucharist service, or equivalent in other church traditions, can be extended to include the offering of seven elements to prepare for the congregation's wider witness to the surrounding community, with prayers for each one. The elements can be presented by members of the congregation and placed on the altar:

- Money: regular tithes and offerings.
- Bread: preferably a home-baked loaf.
- Wine: perhaps a bottle of table wine, rather than the usual Eucharistic wine.
- Soil: a wooden or earthenware bowl of soil.
- Water: in a clear vessel so that it may be seen.
- Seed: a bowl of seeds or a basket of various packaged seeds (members of the congregation can be invited to bring garden seeds to be blessed during the service or the procession).
- Crosses: a basket of small wooden, reed or paper crosses.

Offertory prayers during the Rogation Eucharist

Minister: We pray to you, therefore, Father, to take these gifts of ours;
Ourselves, our lives, our labours, our thoughts, our words, our powers;
Though they all be unworthy to place upon your board
We know you will accept them through Jesus Christ our Lord.

As each element is received, an appropriate prayer is said:

At the presentation of money

Accept, O Lord, our gifts of money, which represent the business of
our daily lives. Use them for the work of your holy church to carry
out your mission; through Jesus Christ our Lord.
Amen.

At the presentation of bread

Almighty God our Saviour, who in the carpenter's shop at Nazareth
laboured for daily bread, accept this bread which is both the fruit
of our work and the satisfaction of our needs, and so bless all our
industry and necessity, for your sake.
Amen.

At the presentation of wine

We offer you, O Lord, this wine, the fruit of the vine. We pray that
you will accept it, that it may become for us the blood of your Son,
Jesus Christ our Lord.
Amen.

At the presentation of soil

Almighty creator, we offer to you this soil in token of the fields and
forests of our land on which we ask your blessing. We ask that the
soil may be wholesome, the crops good, and that we may be faithful
stewards of your mercies, through Jesus Christ our Lord.
Amen.

At the presentation of water

O God, who brought forth life out of the waters of creation, bless
this offering of water and grant that there may be sufficient water to
raise up good crops and to serve the needs of our industries. May we
drink of the living water to bring forth the fruit of godly living from
the soil of our souls, through Jesus Christ our Lord.
Amen.

At the presentation of seeds

O Heavenly Father, who by your wondrous providence made all
grass, herbs and trees, each with seed after its own kind, accept and
bless our offering of seed to be planted throughout our parish, that
the life in all seed sown may burst forth into fulness of its kind,
according to your good creation, and especially the seed of your
Word; through Jesus Christ our Lord.
Amen.

At the presentation of crosses

O God, whose blessed son has promised that we need only to ask in
order to receive, accept and bless these crosses, and grant that in the
fields where we place them they may stand as a sign of our unfailing
trust in your bounty and as encouragement to all who see them to
put their faith in your providence; through Jesus Christ our Lord,
who lives and reigns with you and the Holy Spirit, one God, for ever
and ever.
Amen.

The Rogation procession

*The procession stops at significant places to offer prayer. At each stop
a blessed cross may be fixed to a landmark or set in a cultivated field,
as the minister says:*

Set up your cross, O Lord, as an ensign to the people, and draw all
nations to it.

*A blessing appropriate to each place is then given. Incense can be
burned and the place can be sprinkled with holy water. If a priest
or bishop is not present, the following prayers can be said by a
layperson, adding the words in brackets. The people may also take
blessed crosses and holy water to their homes and use these same
prayers for the hallowing of gardens and farms that are not visited by
the communal procession.*

Blessing of Animals

O God, who created all beasts and cattle in a wonderful order and
gave them into our care: [we ask you to] bless these animals, that
they may be a joy to humankind and sharers in the feeding and
nurture of the world. Make us good shepherds of all your creatures,

we pray, in the name of our merciful and good shepherd, your Son,
our Saviour Jesus Christ.
Amen.

Blessing of Tools

O God, who in your holy word has revealed to us your continual
love and care both in this life and in the life to come: guide and direct
us in our labours here as stewards of your creation. [We ask you to]
bless the tools of our work that by their good use we may bear fruit
to your glory and be diligent in our vocations; in the name of the
Father, and of the Son, and of the Holy Spirit.
Amen.

Blessing of seeds

*If seeds were not blessed at the Eucharist or additional seeds have
been presented for blessing, the offertory prayer may be used to bless
seeds during the procession:*

O Heavenly Father, who by your wondrous providence made all
grass, herbs and trees, each with seed after its own kind, accept and
bless our offering of seed to be planted throughout our parish, that
the life in all seed sown may burst forth into fulness of its kind,
according to your good creation, and especially the seed of your
Word; through Jesus Christ our Lord.
Amen.

Blessing of gardens

O God, who has given each one of us the opportunity to share in the
cultivation of the land: give us also such skill and patience in digging
and sowing and planting that fruit and vegetables and flowers may
sustain our bodies and gladden our hearts by their usefulness and
beauty. [We ask you to] bless with a healthy and plentiful crop this
garden. Endow with skill and endurance those who work here, giving
them rich yields and an assured livelihood; in the name of the Father,
and of the Son, and of the Holy Spirit.
Amen.

Blessing of fields and pastures

O God, who spoke the word and the earth brought forth plants of every kind yielding seed and living creatures of every kind: [we ask you to] bless these pastures and meadows, and all growing grass and green fields; may they remain healthy and unspoiled to the benefit and service of both human and beast. [We ask you also to] bless these fields and all the crops that grow in our countryside; may the soil be wholesome and the crops sound; may the weather be favourable and the workers in good heart. O gracious God, multiply the seed of the sower, the bread of those who eat, and the fruits of righteousness in all your people; in the name of the Father, and of the Son, and of the Holy Spirit.
Amen.

Blessing of orchards

O God, who commanded that the earth bring forth trees bearing fruit of every kind with the seed in it: [we ask you to] bless this orchard, together with the industrious bees who labour in it and the birds who find food and shelter in it; withhold both the late and the early frost that kills, and send in due season such moderate rain and gentle sunshine that we may receive the fruits of it to our strength and to your honour; in the name of the Father, and of the Son, and of the Holy Spirit.
Amen.

Blessing of the parish

The blessing can be given at some central place during the procession, or from the church door

O God our Father, whose Son was content to share the life of his village at Nazareth: [we ask you to] bless the life of this parish with your continual presence. Grant that in every home your name may be hallowed and your will be done, that our people may learn to love every neighbour and live godly lives; through Jesus Christ our Lord, who lives and reigns with you and the Holy Spirit, one God, now and for ever.
Amen.

Reconciliation prayer of St Francis

This prayer and following New Testament reading can be given at a place marking division or parish boundaries, as a reminder of the need for good neighbourly relationships.

Lord, make us instruments of your peace. Where there is hatred, let us sow love; where there is injury, pardon; where there is discord, union; where there is doubt, faith; where there is despair, hope; where there is darkness, light; where there is sadness, joy. Grant that we may not so much seek to be consoled as to console; to be understood as to understand; to be loved as to love. For it is in giving that we receive; it is in pardoning that we are pardoned; and it is in dying that we are born to eternal life.
Amen.

Reconciliation reading: 1 John 4.13–21

By this we know that we abide in him and he in us, because he has given us of his Spirit. And we have seen and do testify that the Father has sent his Son as the Saviour of the world. God abides in those who confess that Jesus is the Son of God, and they abide in God. So we have known and believe the love that God has for us.

God is love, and those who abide in love abide in God, and God abides in them. Love has been perfected among us in this: that we may have boldness on the day of judgement, because as he is, so are we in this world. There is no fear in love, but perfect love casts out fear; for fear has to do with punishment, and whoever fears has not reached perfection in love. We love because he first loved us. Those who say, 'I love God,' and hate their brothers or sisters, are liars; for those who do not love a brother or sister whom they have seen, cannot love God whom they have not seen. The commandment we have from him is this: those who love God must love their brothers and sisters also.

An Elizabethan Rogation Day Service

There are many modern-day Rogation services produced by the main churches. This one combines the merits of great age, an authentic early-modern view of the landscape and an opportunity to hit things with sticks. Something for all the family, one might say.

It has been possible to reconstruct this early Elizabethan ritual through a number of contemporary sources and accounts. The bulk of the text of this ritual is taken from a series of three homilies and an exhortation that were required to be read out at churches undertaking a perambulation, or walk, around the boundaries of the parish during the Monday to Wednesday of Rogation week.[36]

The original homilies are rather long and difficult to follow, but five short passages have been selected to give a sense of the enduring wisdom and relevance of some of these Rogation week traditions and theology. Vestiges of the medieval incantations and prayers for a bountiful harvest can just be discerned through the reformed language. The text has been modernized, and some of the many Bible quotations turned into a full reading, but the underlying message is unchanged.

Although the Elizabethan period, in common with the Reformation generally, was mostly averse to religious processions in the landscape, it is surprising to learn that these perambulations were actually made compulsory. No doubt their practical use as a way of ordering the community overrode any antipathy towards lingering traces of Catholic sympathy for religious processions and pilgrimages, although subsequent injunctions from bishops sought to downplay even further the religious trappings of the procession, such as banning ministers from wearing their surplices.[37]

The procession was to be conducted by the important people of the parish accompanying the curate. There was no closely determined ritual other than to stipulate that the gathering should pause at 'certain convenient places' to hear admonishment, Bible readings and psalm recitations.

There is one specific element of authentic ritual action that survived, which is the use of 'withy wands', or thin supple twigs or rods which children used to 'beat' the bounds during the perambulation. Generally speaking this would occur at a landmark such as a bridge, gate, tree or wall. At the same time, a short pronouncement would be read from Deuteronomy 27.17, which conveniently includes its own responsory: 'Cursed be anyone who moves a neighbour's boundary marker.' All the people shall say, 'Amen!'

The Elizabethan Rogation Service

Psalm 103: Thanksgiving for God's goodness; of David

Minister: Bless the Lord, O my soul,
     and all that is within me,
     bless his holy name.

All: **Bless the Lord, O my soul,**
     and do not forget all his benefits –

     who forgives all your iniquity,
     who heals all your diseases,
     who redeems your life from the Pit,
     who crowns you with steadfast love and mercy,

     who satisfies you with good as long as you live
     so that your youth is renewed like the eagle's.
     The Lord works vindication
     and justice for all who are oppressed.

     He made known his ways to Moses,
     his acts to the people of Israel.
     The Lord is merciful and gracious,
     slow to anger and abounding in steadfast love.

     He will not always accuse,
     nor will he keep his anger forever.
     He does not deal with us according to our sins,
     nor repay us according to our iniquities.

     For as the heavens are high above the earth,
     so great is his steadfast love toward those who fear him;
     as far as the east is from the west,
     so far he removes our transgressions from us.

     As a father has compassion for his children,
     so the Lord has compassion for those who fear him.
     For he knows how we were made;
     he remembers that we are dust.

     As for mortals, their days are like grass;
     they flourish like a flower of the field;
     for the wind passes over it, and it is gone,
     and its place knows it no more.

     But the steadfast love of the Lord is from everlasting to
     everlasting

on those who fear him,
and his righteousness to children's children,
to those who keep his covenant
and remember to do his commandments.

The LORD has established his throne in the heavens,
and his kingdom rules over all.
Bless the Lord, O you his angels,
you mighty ones who do his bidding,
obedient to his spoken word.

Bless the LORD, all his hosts,
his ministers that do his will.
Bless the LORD, all his works,
in all places of his dominion.
Bless the LORD, O my soul.

Cursed be anyone who moves a neighbour's boundary
marker.
Amen.

Homily: Part One

There now follows an exhortation to be spoken to such parishes
where they use their perambulations in Rogation week for the
oversight of the bounds and limits of their towns.

We are now assembled together, good Christian people, principally
to laud and thank almighty God for his great benefits by beholding
the fields replenished with all manner of fruit for the maintenance of
our bodily necessities, for our food and sustenance. Partly also we
will offer our humble prayers to his fatherly providence to conserve
these same fruits, by sending us seasonable weather whereby we
may gather them in to that end for which his merciful goodness has
provided them. And second we have occasion in our walks on these
days to consider the old ancient bounds and limits belonging to our
own township and to our neighbours bordering about us, to the
intent that we should be content with our own and not contentiously
strive for others, to the breach of charity, by encroaching one upon
another, or claiming further than that our forebears have peaceably
laid out unto us for our commodity and comfort in ancient right
and custom. Surely it would be a great oversight by us – who are
Christians in one profession of faith and daily look for that heavenly
inheritance which is bought for every one of us by the blood-shedding

of our Saviour Jesus Christ – to strive and fall out over the earthly bounds of our towns, to the disquiet of our life between ourselves, and to the waste of our goods by vain expenses and costs in the law. We ought to remember that our habitation is but transitory and short in this mortal life. The more shame it would be to fall out into immortal hatred among ourselves for such brittle possessions, and so to lose our eternal inheritance in heaven. It may stand well with charity for a Christian quietly to maintain his or her right and just title; and it is the part of all good inhabitants of the town to preserve, as much as they can, the liberties, franchises, bounds, and limits of their town and country.

Minister: Cursed be anyone who moves a neighbour's boundary marker.
Amen.

Homily: Part Two

Reading: Wisdom 16.24–26

Reader: For creation, serving you who made it,
exerts itself to punish the unrighteous,
and in kindness relaxes on behalf of those who trust in you.
Therefore at that time also, changed into all forms,
it served your all-nourishing bounty,
according to the desire of those who had need,
so that your children, whom you loved, O LORD, might
learn that it is not the production of crops that feeds humankind
but that your word sustains those who trust in you.

Minister: Do not think that God created all this whole world and universe, and then gave it up to be ruled and used after our own wits and devices, taking no more charge over it. God is not like a shipwright who has built his ship to a perfect condition, then delivers it to the mariners and takes no more care for it. Indeed, God has not so created the world that he is careless of it; but he still preserves it by his goodness, he still keeps it in his creation; or else, without his special goodness, it could not stand long in its condition. Therefore St Paul says that he preserves all things and bears them up still in his word, lest they should fall without him once more into the nothingness out of which they were created. If his special goodness were not everywhere present, every creature would be out of order, and no creatures would have their own properties in which they were first created. He is therefore invisibly everywhere and in every creature, and fills both heaven and earth with his presence: in fire, to give heat; in water, to give moisture; in the earth, to give fruit; in the heart, to give strength; indeed in our bread and drink he is, to give us nourishment; where without him the bread and drink cannot give sustenance, nor the herb health. As the wise man plainly confesses it thus: 'it is not the production of crops that feeds humankind but that your word sustains those who trust in you' (Wisd. 16.26). And Moses agrees to the same when he says: 'one does not live by bread alone, but by every word that comes from the mouth of the LORD' (Deut. 8.3). 'For neither herb nor poultice cured them,' says the wise man, 'but it was your word, O LORD, that heals all people' (Wisd. 16.12). It is not therefore the power of the creatures which works their effects, but the goodness of God which works in them. In his word truly do all things consist. By that same word through which heaven and earth were made, by the same are they upheld, maintained, and kept in order, says St Peter, and it shall be until almighty God withdraws his power from them, and speaks their dissolution.

If it were not thus – that the goodness of God is effectually in his creatures to rule them – how could it be that the main sea, so raging and labouring to overflow the earth, could be kept within his bonds and banks, as it is? That holy man Job evidently spied the goodness of God in this point, and confessed, that if he had not a special goodness to the preservation of the earth, it could not be otherwise that the sea would soon overflow it. How could it be that the elements, so diverse and contrary as they are among themselves, should yet agree and abide together in a concord, without destruction one of another, to serve our use, if it comes not only of God's goodness so to temper them? How could the fire not burn and consume all things, if it were left loose to go whither it would, and not kept in its sphere by the goodness of God? Consider the huge substance of the earth, so heavy and great as it is: how could it stand so stably in place as it does, if God's goodness reserved it not so for us to live on? It is you O Lord, says David, who has founded the earth in its stability; and during your word it shall never reel or fall down.

Cursed be anyone who moves a neighbour's boundary marker.
Amen.

Homily: Part Three

Reading: Jeremiah 9.23–24

Reader: Thus says the LORD: Do not let the wise boast in their wisdom, do not let the mighty boast in their might, do not let the wealthy boast in their wealth; but let those who are boastful boast in this, that they understand and know me, that I am the LORD; I act with steadfast love, justice, and righteousness in the earth, for in these things I delight, says the LORD.

Minister: In his power we will have sufficient ability to know our duty to God. In him we will be comforted and encouraged to walk in our duty. In him shall we be fitting vessels to receive the grace of almighty God. For it is he that purges and purifies the mind by his secret working, and he only is present everywhere by his invisible power, and contains all things in his dominion. He lightens the heart to conceive worthy thoughts of almighty God. He sits on the tongue of men and women to stir them to speak his honour. No language is hidden from him, for he has knowledge of all speech. Only he ministers spiritual strength to the powers of our soul and body. To hold to the way which God has prepared for us, to walk rightly in our journey, we must acknowledge that it is in the power of his Spirit which helps our infirmity. That we may boldly come in prayer, and call upon almighty God as our father, it is by this Holy Spirit, who makes intercession for us with continual sighs. If we have any gift, with which we may work to the glory of God and benefit of our neighbour, all is wrought by this one same Spirit who is distributed to every person individually. If we have any wisdom it is not from ourselves: we cannot glory in it as something that began in ourselves; but we ought to glory in God, from whom it came to us, as the prophet wrote: 'but let those who are boastful boast in this, that they understand and know me, that I am the LORD; I act with steadfast love, justice, and righteousness in the earth, for in these things I delight, says the LORD' (Jer. 9.24). This wisdom can only be attained by the direction of the Spirit of God, and therefore it is called spiritual wisdom.

Cursed be anyone who moves a neighbour's boundary marker.
Amen.

Homily: Part Four

Reading: Romans 1.19–22

Reader: For what can be known about God is plain to them, because God has shown it to them. Ever since the creation of the world his eternal power and divine nature, invisible though they are, have been understood and seen through the things he has made. So they are without excuse; for though they knew God, they did not honour him as God or give thanks to him, but they became futile in their thinking, and their senseless minds were darkened. Claiming to be wise, they became fools.

Minister: I am purposed this day, good devout Christian people, to declare to you the most deserved praise and commendation of almighty God. First of all in consideration of the marvellous creation of this world, or for the conservation and governance thereof, wherein his great power and wisdom might excellently appear, to move us to honour and dread him. But also in consideration of his liberal and large goodness, which he daily bestows on us, his reasonable creatures, for whose sake he made this whole universal world with all the commodities and goods therein: which his singular goodness, well and diligently remembered on our part, should dutifully move us with hearty affection to love him, and with word and deed to praise him and serve him all the days of our life. Only I would wish your affection inflamed unseen within yourself to raise up some motion of thanksgiving to the goodness of almighty God in every such point as shall be opened. For else what shall it avail us to hear and know the great goodness of God towards us, to know that whatever is good proceeds from him, as from the principal fountain and the only author, or to know that whatever is sent from him must needs be good and wholesome, if the hearing of such matter moves us no further than simply to know about it? What good did it do the wise men of the world to have a knowledge of the power and divinity of God by the secret inspiration of him, when they did not honour and glorify him in such knowledge as God? What praise was it to them, by the consideration of the creation of the world to behold his goodness, and yet were not thankful to him again for his creation?

Cursed be anyone who moves a neighbour's boundary marker.
Amen.

Homily: Part Five

Reading: Proverbs 3.3–10

Reader: Do not let loyalty and faithfulness forsake you;
        bind them around your neck,
        write them on the tablet of your heart.
        So you will find favour and good repute
        in the sight of God and of people.
        Trust in the LORD with all your heart,
        and do not rely on your own insight.
        In all your ways acknowledge him,
        and he will make straight your paths.
        Do not be wise in your own eyes;
        fear the LORD, and turn away from evil.
        It will be a healing for your flesh
        and a refreshment for your body.
        Honour the LORD with your substance
        and with the first fruits of all your produce;
        then your barns will be filled with plenty,
        and your vats will be bursting with wine.

Minister: So if you now want to have your prayers heard before almighty God – for the increase of your corn and cattle, and for the defence thereof from unseasonable mists and blasts, from hail and other such tempests – then love equity and righteousness, and pursue mercy and charity, which God requires most of all from us. Almighty God respected this chiefly when making his civil laws for his people the Israelites, charging farm owners not to gather up their corn too completely at harvest season, nor the grapes and olives in gathering time, but to leave behind some ears of corn for the poor gleaners. By this he meant to induce them to pity the poor, to relieve the needy, to show mercy and kindness. Nothing is wasted which for his sake is distributed to the poor. For he who ministers seed to the sower and bread to the hungry, who sends down the first and subsequent rains upon your fields to fill up the barns with corn and the winepresses with wine and oil – he, I say, who recompenses all kind good deeds by the resurrection of the just – he will assuredly recompense all merciful deeds shown to the needy however unable are the poor people upon whom they are bestowed. As Solomon says: 'Do not let loyalty and faithfulness forsake you; bind them around your neck, write them on the tablet of your heart. So you will find favour and good repute in the sight of God and of people ... [Thus] honour the LORD with your substance and with the first fruits of all your produce; then your barns will be filled with plenty, and your vats will be bursting with wine' (Prov. 3.3–4, 9–10). Indeed God has promised to open the windows of heaven for the liberal righteous person, that they shall want nothing. He will repress the devouring caterpillar, which would devour your fruits. He will give you peace and quiet to gather in your harvest, that every one of you 'shall all sit under their own vines' (Micah 4.4) quietly, without fear of those foreign enemies invading you. He will give you not only food to feed on, but stomachs and good appetites to take comfort of your harvest, whereby in all things you may have a sufficiency. Finally, he will bless you with all manner of abundance in this transitory life, and endue you with all manner of benediction in the next world, in the kingdom of heaven, through the merits of our Lord and Saviour. To whom with the Father and the Holy Spirit be all honour everlastingly. Amen.

Cursed be anyone who moves a neighbour's boundary marker.
Amen.

Blessing of a Bridge, Road and Other Means of Transport: Roman Catholic Order

Communal facilities for all forms of transportation can be held up with this special service of blessing. It has been prepared by the Roman Catholic Church, which advises that any service should involve members of the local community in whose interest the infrastructure of travel has been created and is maintained. Bridges, roads and other highways are a particular form of outdoor space which bring communities together, and which have special considerations over the safety of their users.

This service is reproduced by kind permission of the International Commission on English in the Liturgy, and can also be found in the *Book of Blessings*.[38]

Blessing of Means of Transportation

An introductory song or hymn can be sung

Minister: In the name of the Father, and of the Son, and of the Holy Spirit.

All make the sign of the cross and reply:

All: **Amen.**

With one heart and one mind let us bless the Lord Jesus Christ, who is the way, the truth, and the life. Blessed be God now and for ever.
Amen.

Christ, the Son of God, came into the world to gather those who were scattered. Whatever contributes to bringing us closer together therefore is in accord with God's plan. Thus those who are separated from each other by mountains, oceans, or great distances are brought nearer to each other whenever new highways are built or other means of transportation developed.

Let us, then, call on God to bless those who have worked on this project and to protect with his gracious help those who will make use of it.

Reading

Reader: Brothers and sisters, listen to the words of the holy Gospel according to John (John 14.6–7): I am the way, the truth, and the life.
Jesus said to Thomas, 'I am the way, and the truth, and the life. No one comes to the Father except through me. If you know me, you will know my Father also. From now on you do know him and have seen him.'

Psalm 23

Minister: The response to the psalm is: 'Guide me, O Lord, in right paths.'
Guide me, O Lord, in right paths.

The Lord is my shepherd, I shall not want.
He makes me lie down in green pastures;
he leads me beside still waters;
he restores my soul.
Guide me, O Lord, in right paths.

Even though I walk through the darkest valley,
I fear no evil; for you are with me;
your rod and your staff –
they comfort me.
Guide me, O Lord, in right paths.

You prepare a table before me
in the presence of my enemies;
you anoint my head with oil;
my cup overflows.
Guide me, O Lord, in right paths.

Surely goodness and mercy shall follow me
all the days of my life,
and I shall dwell in the house of the LORD
my whole life long.
Guide me, O LORD, in right paths.

Intercessions

Minister: Let us join together in prayer to the Lord Jesus Christ, who is the way for us to reach our eternal homeland, saying:
Guide our steps along your way, O Lord.

Assisting
Minister: Lord Jesus, you went from town to town preaching your Gospel and healing the sick; may you still pass along our streets and highways and with your compassion give us strength. For this we pray:
Guide our steps along your way, O Lord.

Lord Jesus, when your disciples were on the waters of the lake, you were there to rescue them from every peril; be with us amid the storms of this world. For this we pray:
Guide our steps along your way, O Lord.

Lord Jesus, you became a companion to your disciples on the road to Emmaus; bless us on our journeys and warm our hearts by your words. For this we pray:
Guide our steps along your way, O Lord.

Lord Jesus, when you ascended into heaven, you showed the way for us; bear us up in our earthly pilgrimage, so that we may have a dwelling place in your Father's house. For this we pray:
Guide our steps along your way, O Lord.

Lord Jesus, you gave us to your Mother to be her children; through her intercession make our journey safe, so that some day we may see you and for ever rejoice with you. For this we pray:
Guide our steps along your way, O Lord.

The prayers of blessing

A minister who is a priest or deacon says the prayer of blessing with hands outstretched; a lay minister says the prayer with hands joined.

A Blessing of a bridge, highway, street, railway, or airport

O God, you are never far off from those who serve you; with fatherly protection you always guard those who trust in you. By your grace be the guide going before those who use this [bridge, highway, street, railway, airport] and be the companion to sustain them on their way. By your favour protect them from adversity, so that they may arrive safely at their destination and accomplish what they set out to do. We ask this through Christ our Lord.
Amen.

B Blessing of a bridge, highway, street, railway, or airport

O God of boundless mercy and majesty, neither distance nor time separates you from those you watch over. In every place stay close to your servants who trust in you, and wherever they go be their leader and companion. Let no adversity harm them nor any obstacle hinder them on their way. Make all things work for their well-being and true benefit, so that whatever they rightly desire they may successfully achieve. We ask this through Christ our Lord.
Amen.

Concluding rite

May the Lord be the guide on our journeys, so that we may travel in peace and reach eternal life.
Amen.

A concluding hymn can be sung

Prayers for Street Pastors

The following three prayers have been kindly provided by the Ascension Trust, a UK charity which helps to fund and promote the work of Street Pastors.[39] The trust is an inter-denominational Christian organization which has a particular focus on serving and witnessing to wider society, particularly those who are marginalized, disadvantaged or vulnerable. These prayers are, of course, only for use after formal Street Pastor training, details of which are in the endnote on page 224.

The Ascension Trust is the governing body for the Street Pastor initiative, which operates across the UK and internationally to provide help and support to those out on the streets, particularly during the evenings. It began in 2003 in Brixton, London, and currently has a presence in over 240 towns in Britain. The prayers reproduced below demonstrate the focus of Street Pastors, a modern development of the idea of outdoor Christian ritual that perfectly demonstrates the adaptability of long-standing Christian traditions to new challenges and social changes. They include a prayer of declaration, focusing on the intentions of the Street Pastors and the needs of the community they will be serving, a prayer of commissioning which is read over new Street Pastors, and a responsorial prayer.

Street Pastors' Prayer Declaration

'For a child is born to us, a son is given to us. The government will rest on his shoulders, and he will be called: Wonderful Counsellor, Mighty God, Everlasting Father, Prince of Peace. Of the increase of his government and of peace there will be no end.' (Isa. 9.6–7, NLT)

Lord Jesus, we thank you for this promise in your word of the increase of your Kingdom. We rejoice that your Kingdom will never stop growing!

We praise you that your rule is always accompanied by peace, shalom peace, fullness of well-being.

We declare that as we, your people, seek first your kingdom with all our hearts, everything that this land needs for peace will be released from heaven.

We call to the people of our land: 'Hear the word of the LORD and turn again to him' so that in every corner of the land many would turn, be forgiven and cleansed, healed and delivered, and find life!

We declare peace over our land – not the kind of peace that the world gives – but the mighty, lasting, life-transforming peace that Jesus gives.

We speak the peace of Jesus into households and families; we speak the peace of Jesus into communities, we speak the peace of Jesus into towns and cities right across the land, with the longing that many people would recognize and respond to the Prince of Peace.

And we call for a great turning of hearts to follow Jesus, to recognize again the holiness and the righteousness of our great God, who has created and blessed this land and been so merciful to us through the generations.

Let this land shine out among the nations with the radiant peace of a nation governed by the Most High King.
Amen.

Street Pastors' Commissioning Prayer

God our Father, as disciples of Jesus we accept our commissioning from you to invest our lives in others, and we now ask that you give these Street Pastors the power, wisdom and courage to live out the Kingdom life as they patrol the streets of our town.

May Jesus be seen in their lives as they provide care, practical help and a listening ear while on patrol and may they always and everywhere model the life of Christ with authenticity and great zeal.

Open their eyes and ears to see and hear the needs of our night-time economy, which you have called and equipped these Street Pastors to meet.

Father, as your Son modelled for us what it means to be a servant by washing the feet of the disciples, may they exhibit a servant attitude in all they do as Street Pastors on the streets of our town.

May you be their Lord, light and guardian as they undertake the work of Street Pastors, that you have called them to. Grant them perseverance when tired, that they would not grow weary in doing well.

We commission them into your service, in Jesus' name.
Amen.

Street Pastors' Commissioning Prayer: Responses

Do you acknowledge God's call on your life to serve him as a Street Pastor here in this town?
We do.

Do you acknowledge your dependence of Jesus Christ in the power of the Holy Spirit as you serve as a Street Pastor?
We do.

Do you seek with his help to demonstrate the love of Jesus Christ in word and deed on the streets of this town?
We do.

Do you promise to serve as a Street Pastor in accordance with the policies determined by the trustees?
We do.

On the basis of your responses to these questions it is now my privilege and delight to commission you as Street Pastors.

Blessing of a Sports Field or Gymnasium:
Roman Catholic Order

Physical activity is good for both mental and physical health, as this service takes care to emphasize in its introduction and blessing. The service is presented here as one suited to any form of sports or playing field, and in its original conception has also been designed for indoor facilities such as a gymnasium.

The communal nature of all sports is an important dimension of the gathering for this service, and it is intended to include players and participants and also those who will manage or staff the site. This service is reproduced by kind permission of the International Commission on English in the Liturgy, and can also be found in the *Book of Blessings*.[40]

Blessing of a Sports Field or Playing Field

An introductory song or hymn can be sung

Celebrant: In the name of the Father, and of the Son, and of the Holy Spirit.

All make the sign of the cross and reply:

All: **Amen.**

May God, the source and origin of all, from whom every good thing comes to us, be with you all. **And with your spirit.**

God has given us our physical powers in order that we may serve him joyously, help one another, and, by discipline in accord with the law of God, make our body fit for every good work. God therefore approves of recreation for the relaxation of the mind and the exercise of the body. Care of our bodies fosters mental well-being, and we more readily establish friendly and affable relations with other people.

Reading

Reader: Brothers and sisters, listen to the words of the first letter of Paul to the Corinthians (1 Cor. 9.24–27): Run so as to win.

Do you not know that in a race the runners all compete, but only one receives the prize? Run in such a way that you may win it. Athletes exercise self-control in all things; they do it to receive a perishable wreath, but we an imperishable one. So I do not run aimlessly, nor do I box as though beating the air; but I punish my body and enslave it, so that after proclaiming to others I myself should not be disqualified.

Psalm 100

Celebrant: The response to the psalm is: 'We are his people: the sheep of his flock.'
We are his people, the sheep of his flock.

Make a joyful noise to the LORD, all the earth.
Worship the LORD with gladness;
come into his presence with singing.
We are his people, the sheep of his flock.

Know that the LORD is God.
It is he that made us, and we are his;
we are his people, and the sheep of his pasture.
We are his people, the sheep of his flock.

Enter his gates with thanksgiving,
and his courts with praise.
Give thanks to him, bless his name.
We are his people, the sheep of his flock.

For the LORD is good;
his steadfast love endures forever,
and his faithfulness to all generations.
We are his people, the sheep of his flock.

Intercessions

Celebrant: The Lord Jesus, our strength and our joy, calls all human beings to himself, so that all who are weary and find life burdensome may be refreshed by walking in his love. Therefore let us call on him with trust, saying:
Lord Jesus, draw us to yourself.

Assisting Minister: You are the life of all those you redeemed by your blood.
Lord Jesus, draw us to yourself.

You are the strength of the weak and the prize of the strong.
Lord Jesus, draw us to yourself.

You went about doing good and healing all ills.
Lord Jesus, draw us to yourself.

You sent your Spirit to be the Comforter who sustains us.
Lord Jesus, draw us to yourself.

You have made love for you and for one another the source of true joy.
Lord Jesus, draw us to yourself.

You heed our prayer that our joy may be full.
Lord Jesus, draw us to yourself.

You want us to be of one heart and one mind in you.
Lord Jesus, draw us to yourself.

Prayer of blessing

With hands outstretched, the celebrant says:

Lord, we sing your praises without ceasing.
You rule over all things with wonderful order,
you temper the cares and burdens of our toil,
and, by giving us rest and healthy recreation,
you refresh our weary bodies and minds.
We entreat your kindness,
that this place and its facilities
will contribute to leisure activities
that renew the spirit and strengthen mind and body.
Grant that all who meet here may find
the enrichment of companionship
and together offer you the praise that is your due.
We ask this through Christ our Lord.
Amen.

Hymn

The celebrant sprinkles those present and the site with holy water, while a suitable song or hymn is sung

Concluding rite

With hands outstretched over those present, the celebrant concludes the rite by saying:

> May God who brings light to our minds and strength to our bodies guide us in all we do, so that each day we may find gladness and friendship.
> **Amen.**

The celebrant blesses all present

> And may almighty God bless you, the Father, and the Son, and the Holy Spirit.
> **Amen.**

A concluding hymn can be sung

Visiting a Cemetery: Roman Catholic Order

This order is a formal and solemn ritual to commemorate the departed who are buried in a cemetery. It is designed for use on All Souls Day (2 November), Remembrance Day or Remembrance Sunday, or on the anniversary of the death or burial of a particular person. It is also suited to mark when a gravestone or other monument is erected. It could be used at the end of a church Mass or as a standalone act of worship.

It can also be adapted for use by individual groups when they go to visit a grave, a ritual to aid mourning and remembrance alike. The form that follows has been designed for use by a priest, deacon or lay minister, or in the case of private group by a member of the family visiting. The service is reproduced by kind permission of the International Commission on English in the Liturgy, and can also be found in the *Book of Blessings*, which also has other services for blessing a cemetery.[41]

Order for Visiting a Cemetery

Minister: Praise be to God our Father, who raised Jesus Christ from the dead. Blessed be God for ever.

All: **Blessed be God for ever.**

My dear friends, we gather today to pray for our brothers and sisters whose bodies lie here in rest. They have passed from death to life in company with the Lord Jesus, who died and rose to new life, and are purified now of their faults. We pray that God may welcome them among all the saints of heaven.

Reading

Reader: Brothers and sisters, listen to the words of the first letter of Paul to the Thessalonians (1 Thess. 4.13–18): We shall stay with the Lord for ever.

But we do not want you to be uninformed, brothers and sisters, about those who have died, so that you may not grieve as others do who have no hope. For since we believe that Jesus died and rose again, even so, through Jesus, God will bring with him those who have died. For this we declare to you by the word of the Lord, that we who are alive, who are left until the coming of the Lord, will by no means precede those who have died. For the Lord himself, with a cry of command, with the archangel's call and with the sound of God's trumpet, will descend from heaven, and the dead in Christ will rise first. Then we who are alive, who are left, will be caught up in the clouds together with them to meet the Lord in the air; and so we will be with the Lord forever. Therefore encourage one another with these words.

Psalm 25

Minister: The response to the psalm is: 'To you, O LORD, I lift up my soul.'
To you, O LORD, I lift up my soul.

O my God, in you I trust; do not let me be put to shame;
do not let my enemies exult over me.
Do not let those who wait for you be put to shame;
let them be ashamed who are wantonly treacherous.
To you, O LORD, I lift up my soul.

Make me to know your ways, O LORD;
teach me your paths.
Lead me in your truth, and teach me,
for you are the God of my salvation;
for you I wait all day long.
To you, O LORD, I lift up my soul.

Be mindful of your mercy, O LORD, and of your
steadfast love,
for they have been from of old.
Do not remember the sins of my youth or my transgressions;
according to your steadfast love remember me,
for your goodness' sake, O LORD!
To you, O LORD, I lift up my soul.

Good and upright is the Lord;
therefore he instructs sinners in the way.
He leads the humble in what is right,
and teaches the humble his way.
To you, O Lord, I lift up my soul.

All the paths of the Lord are steadfast love and
faithfulness,
for those who keep his covenant and his decrees.
For your name's sake, O Lord,
pardon my guilt, for it is great.
To you, O Lord, I lift up my soul.

Litany

*While the litany is recited the minister may sprinkle the graves with
holy water, and incense them if desired too*

Lord, have mercy
Lord, have mercy

Christ, have mercy
Christ, have mercy

Lord, have mercy
Lord, have mercy

Holy Mary, Mother of God
pray for them

Saint Michael
pray for them

Saint John the Baptist
pray for them

Saint Joseph
pray for them

Saint Peter
pray for them

Saint Paul
pray for them

Saint Andrew
pray for them

Saint Stephen
pray for them

Saint Ann
pray for them

Saint Teresa
pray for them

Saint Catherine
pray for them

The names of other saints may be added

All holy men and women
pray for them

Christ, pardon all their faults
Lord, hear our prayer

Christ, remember the good they have done
Lord, hear our prayer

Christ, receive them into eternal life
Lord, hear our prayer

Christ, comfort all those who mourn
Lord, hear our prayer

Lord, have mercy
Lord, have mercy

Christ, have mercy
Christ, have mercy

Lord, have mercy
Lord, have mercy

The Lord's Prayer

With Christ there is mercy and fullness of redemption; let us pray as
Jesus taught us:
Our Father ...

Prayer

Either
All-powerful God, whose mercy is never withheld from those who
call upon you in hope, look kindly on your servants (*names*), who
departed this life confessing your name, and number them among
your saints for evermore.

We ask this through Christ our Lord.
Amen.

Or

Almighty God and Father, by the mystery of the cross, you have made us strong; by the sacrament of the resurrection you have sealed us as your own. Look kindly upon your servants, now freed from the bonds of mortality, and count them among your saints in heaven.

We ask this through Christ our Lord.
Amen.

Or for one person

Almighty God and Father, it is our certain faith that your Son, who died on the cross, was raised from the dead, the first fruits of all who have fallen asleep. Grant that through this mystery your servant [*name*], who has gone to his/her rest in Christ, may share in the joy of his resurrection.

We ask this through Christ our Lord.
Amen.

Or for the blessing of a gravestone or monument

O God, by whose mercy the faithful departed find rest, bless this gravestone with which we mark the resting place of [*name*]. May he/she have everlasting life and rejoice in you with your saints for ever.

We ask this through Christ our Lord.
Amen.

Concluding rite

Eternal rest grant unto them, O Lord.
And let perpetual light shine upon them.

May they rest in peace.
Amen.

May their souls and the souls of the faithful departed, through the mercy of God, rest in peace.
Amen.

A concluding hymn can be sung

4

WATER BLESSINGS AND RITUALS

Water is the primal element of creation. Without water there is no life, a significance of the most basic biological fact, and one that fully justifies the ocean's place in the Bible's opening sentence. From the waters of Chaos to the crossing of the Jordan, and its re-crossing with the baptismal mission of John the Baptist, water ripples with spiritual energy through all parts of the Hebrew Bible and the New Testament alike. It still surrounds us today and can greatly enhance environmental, psychological and community well-being, in addition to serving as a medium for the most powerful spiritual connections and rituals.

The liturgies in this chapter reflect a wide range of interactions with natural water features of every kind. From the blessing of springs and wells through to Epiphany celebrations, river liturgies and sea and ocean services, there are many ways in which water can bring people together in celebration and praise. As an environmental gesture there can be little more powerful than the sense of human dependence on water, and thanksgiving for its ever-flowing bounty.

There are also many rituals that highlight the perils of its contamination, a spiritual expression that echoes greatly today. Many of these older rituals refer to a shadow lurking in the depths, demonic powers and possessions, the potential for harm, the most unruly of elements resistant to full human control. Today it might seem like we have mostly conquered the dangers of waters, but that is to highlight quite another problem again: human pollution. Where once liturgies spoke of spiritual contamination sullying the pure waters of creation, we can now replace that with a more literal kind of contamination, as we confront the huge problem of plastic pollution in every part of our watercourses.

In a secular and sceptical age it might be said that saying a blessing over a polluted watercourse will not solve the underlying problem, but that would be to misunderstand the most powerful human dimension of ritual. By shaping our highest values and most intense expressions of concern into an important communal shape and language we can give voice to something that ripples far beyond its immediate action. To think in terms of an unsullied creation now marred by human failure, weakness and laziness has much to commend it from any perspective. Indeed the word sin seems eminently appropriate when considering sea life choking to death on plastic rubbish.

In terms of the human benefits of aquatic environments, they are also places of rest and refreshment. Still waters offer a salve for troubled thoughts, recognized as a place of natural healing by psychologists and counsellors. The effects of being by natural water, blue therapy as it is sometimes known, are pronounced and measurable. But such data is nothing new to those steeped in the ancient wisdom of the scriptures, who are powerfully aware of the potential of water to heal and to remake, to cleanse to the point of rebirth.

One of the practices of the Celtic church was to 'sing psalms to the sound of the waves', as Bede puts it in his *Life of St Cuthbert*. Many of the earliest hermit rituals around water are too intense and solitary to include in this book, but one thing does present itself as a possible ritual accompaniment that modern congregations can revive.[42] For any sort of seashore service, the sound of breaking waves could be used to punctuate the words of the gathering, the beat of the sea itself joining in a song of praise. When performed beside the sea, any of the psalms and songs in this chapter therefore might pause between verses to take their beat from the ocean itself by waiting for a wave to break: a timeless rhythm unaltered since the dawn of creation.

Well Blessing from the *Bobbio Missal*

Celtic spirituality is much celebrated in the modern church, held up as an expression of religion that has a particular sympathy towards the natural world. Despite the modern revival, however, there is little authentic, early Celtic material that is currently available for churches to use today. All of which makes the following blessing a particularly important artefact which has been recovered and translated here for the first time in a modern service book, a piece of authentic landscape spirituality reflecting Celtic traditions.[43]

This text is a well blessing, for a naturally occurring flow or gathering of water, and as such could be directed towards any natural body of water, including the rivers from where water is still extracted to this day for supplying our homes: 70 per cent of London's drinking water comes from the Thames. The comment about protecting our water sources from pollution could not be more relevant.

It appears in an early liturgical text called the *Bobbio Missal*, which was compiled some time in the seventh century, probably in what is now modern-day France. Scholars have suggested it bears the imprint of the Irish missionary St Columbanus. The text has similarities with other north European texts (known collectively as Gallican rites), which set them apart as a family from more Roman-influenced liturgies.

The Well Blessing

Holy Lord, Father, Almighty God,
who by your own divinity taught our ancestors Abraham, Isaac
    and Jacob
to dig out wells from the rock and to drink water from them,
we humbly beseech you to answer these prayers
that you sanctify the waters of this well
to the health, use and heavenly blessing of this community
that fleeing all temptations of the devil
or incursion of pollution
whoever drinks from them
might receive the blessing of our Lord Jesus Christ
Amen.

Three Anglo-Saxon Water Prayers

These three prayers over water are taken from an eighth-century liturgical book, the *Pontifical of St Egbert*, named after an archbishop of York who died in AD 766.[44] All three demonstrate a clear belief in the power of water to hold a spiritual 'charge', even to the point of harbouring demons and diabolical powers. By the same token water is also seen as a vehicle for conveying good health and blessing.

The first prayer is clearly the most resonant in a modern setting, a blessing for water which has been tainted by human 'negligence', which could refer to neglect or to an act of pollution. It is designed for prayer over a naturally flowing spring, and as with the well blessing from the *Bobbio Missal*, see page 97, it seems entirely applicable to any watercourse.

The second is an exorcism over the 'creature' of water, a striking reminder that water is part of God's creation. It envisions that the water redeemed by this formula can be carried away for use 'in the home or field', indicating traditions common in early medieval Britain. It appears to be designed for use within a church building, taking a ritual blessing out into the landscape thereafter, but hints at an alternative, non-church setting.

The final ritual is a blessing formula that almost serves as a follow-up to the exorcism, referring to water that has already been 'prepared in many ways for purifications'. Once again it refers to the blessed water being sprinkled wherever the people see fit to use it, powerful against both harmful spiritual powers and also diseases.

1 A Prayer Over a Spring Where the Water Has Been Affected by Negligence

Holy Lord, Almighty Father, Eternal God, who through the power of your invisibility has offered these waters to be founded from nothing in their material form, and from the hidden unsearchable hollows has set flowing the stream for this spring through the magnificent abyss, by your grace for the use of humanity, we your servants pray and beseech you, work on these waters which negligence [*insert here the particular form of pollution*] has polluted, and recall them to wholeness by the grace of your Holy Spirit.

And may the spring be pure and may the spirit of the cunning enemy depart that these waters thus sanctified may be drinkable by your family, and that the waters may sanctify body and heart through Jesus Christ our Lord, who with the Father and Holy Spirit is worshipped and glorified, one God now and forever.
Amen.

2 An Exorcism of Water

I exorcise you, creature water, in the name of God the Father Almighty and in the name of his Son, Jesus Christ and the Holy Spirit, so that all power of the adversary and all invasion of the devil, all phantasms and all power of the enemy be eradicated and flee from this creature of water.

Whence I exorcise you, creature of water, through the living God, through the true God, through the holy God and through our Lord Jesus Christ that you may be made holy water, blessed water so that wherever you are sprinkled or aspersed – whether in the home or in the field – you may send out all phantasms and all power of the enemy. So I consecrate this holy water. May it promote the dedication of this church [*or whatever thing the devotion of the faithful wish to use it for*] and through it and through the divine benediction with the help of the Lord, whether through mouth or by hand, may this house of the Lord God [*or other thing*] be consecrated to our office and be to us divine through the grace of the Holy Spirit. And may they be permanently consecrated to the perpetual invocation of the name of the Lord, and may the Holy Spirit make her home in them through Jesus Christ our Lord, who with the Father and Holy Spirit is worshipped and glorified, one God now and forever.
Amen.

3 A Blessing of Water

God who has founded the great substance and sacrament of the
waters to the health of humanity, be present by our invocations and
with this element prepared in many ways for purifications, establish
the power of your blessing that the creatures serving you in your
mysteries may have demons sent away and diseases sent back from
them. And may you grant the effect of divine grace that in our
homes or other places of the faithful on whatever these are sprinkled
they may cure the foulness of all things, and may free them from
corruption. May all the insidious lurking enemy be sent out and
whatever also looks enviously on those having safety or quietness
may be sent away by the aspersion of these waters so that the health
received through the invocation of your name may be defended from
all assaults. Through Jesus Christ our Lord, who with the Father and
Holy Spirit is worshipped and glorified, one God now and forever.
Amen.

The Great Blessing of the Waters

Church ritual flows quite literally into the landscape with this most ancient and powerful liturgy used to mark the baptism of Christ in the River Jordan. It has been and remains a cornerstone of the Orthodox Christian year, which celebrates it as the Feast of Theophany on 6 January. Although the liturgy is sometimes conducted inside the church building beside the font, it is also commonly held outside using natural water, by a river, holy well, lake or even the sea.

The priest brings a hand-held cross to the water, immersing it three times during the ritual. In some Greek traditions the priest will throw a metal cross into the sea, whereupon the youths of the village dive in and compete to be the first to find it and bring it to the surface. In Russia, where the weather in January precludes such spiritual athleticism, many churches prepare for this liturgy with a chainsaw, cutting a cross-shaped hole in the ice to allow the faithful to line up and immerse themselves three times. Due to a 13-day difference between Eastern and Western church calendars the service in Russia is actually held on 19 January.

From the earliest church onwards, great emphasis has been placed on the significance of Jesus' baptism in the River Jordan. Jesus, the Son of God, is without sin, yet undergoes a ritual of repentance. This seeming paradox is resolved with the interpretation that this moment embodies Jesus' full descent into the created world, the Creator God entering into and operating across all levels of creation, blessing and sanctifying the very elements of the universe. On this day, therefore, the Orthodox church teaches that all water becomes holy, signifying the redemption of nothing less than the whole of creation itself. As a ritual centred on the landscape, it is therefore replete with biblical texts, prayers and theological interpretations that wholeheartedly embrace the natural world.

The Great Blessing is to some extent based on the liturgy used for baptism, and some of the language and actions may be familiar to traditions outside the Orthodox church. The feast has been celebrated since at least the early third century, and the form of words reproduced here is ascribed to St Sophronius, who was patriarch of Jerusalem from AD 634 to 638. This text is based on two traditional translations of St Sophronius' ritual, it is not an authorized text issued by any church.[45] Numerous variations can be found online, and as with all rituals do be sure to follow guidance from your own church traditions and leadership. No better final recommendation can be given than to suggest joining your own nearest Orthodox Christian community in January to participate in this timeless outdoor ritual.

The Order of the Great Sanctification on the Holy Theophany

The minister leads the congregation to the place of blessing the waters, carrying a hand cross. It is traditional that the Gospel book is also carried in this procession. In Orthodox tradition some of the liturgy is sung by a choir, and without such an arrangement we suggest the words could be said by the gathered faithful.

All: The voice of the Lord cries upon the waters saying, O come, and all receive the spirit of wisdom, the spirit of understanding, the spirit of the fear of God, even Christ, who is made manifest. (*Said three times*)
Today the nature of water is sanctified, and the Jordan is divided, and rolls back the flowing of its waters, beholding the baptism of the Lord. (*Said twice*).
As a man you came to the river, O Christ the King, desiring to receive the baptism of a servant, O good one, at the hand of John the Forerunner, because of our sins, O lover of humankind. (*Said twice*).
Glory to the Father, and to the Son, and to the Holy Spirit, now, and ever, and unto ages of ages. Amen.

Minister: To the voice crying in the wilderness, 'Prepare the way of the Lord', you came, O Lord, taking the form of a servant and asking for baptism, though you know not sin. The waters beheld you, and were afraid. The Forerunner began trembling and cried, 'How shall the lamp of light be lighted? How shall the servant lay hands on his Lord? Sanctify me and the waters, O Saviour, you who take away the sins of the world.'

Deacon: Wisdom!

Reader: The parable from the prophecy of Isaiah 35.1–10

Deacon: Let us attend.

Reader:
The wilderness and the dry land shall be glad,
    the desert shall rejoice and blossom;
like the crocus it shall blossom abundantly,
    and rejoice with joy and singing.
The glory of Lebanon shall be given to it,
    the majesty of Carmel and Sharon.
They shall see the glory of the LORD,
    the majesty of our God.
Strengthen the weak hands,
    and make firm the feeble knees.
Say to those who are of a fearful heart,
    'Be strong, do not fear!
Here is your God.
    He will come with vengeance,
with terrible recompense.
    He will come and save you.'
Then the eyes of the blind shall be opened,
    and the ears of the deaf unstopped;
then the lame shall leap like a deer,
    and the tongue of the speechless sing for joy.
For waters shall break forth in the wilderness,
    and streams in the desert;
the burning sand shall become a pool,
    and the thirsty ground springs of water;
the haunt of jackals shall become a swamp,
    the grass shall become reeds and rushes.
A highway shall be there,
    and it shall be called the Holy Way;
the unclean shall not travel on it,
    but it shall be for God's people;
    no traveller, not even fools, shall go astray.
No lion shall be there,
    nor shall any ravenous beast come up on it;

they shall not be found there,
    but the redeemed shall walk there.
And the ransomed of the LORD shall return,
    and come to Zion with singing;
everlasting joy shall be upon their heads;
    they shall obtain joy and gladness,
    and sorrow and sighing shall flee away.

Deacon: Wisdom!

Reader: A reading from the prophecy of Isaiah 55.1–13.

Deacon: Let us attend.

Reader: Ho, everyone who thirsts,
    come to the waters;
and you that have no money,
    come, buy and eat!
Come, buy wine and milk
    without money and without price.
Why do you spend your money for that which is not bread,
    and your labour for that which does not satisfy?
Listen carefully to me, and eat what is good,
    and delight yourselves in rich food.
Incline your ear, and come to me;
    listen, so that you may live.
I will make with you an everlasting covenant,
    my steadfast, sure love for David.
See, I made him a witness to the peoples,
    a leader and commander for the peoples.
See, you shall call nations that you do not know,
    and nations that do not know you shall run to you,
because of the LORD your God, the Holy One of Israel,
    for he has glorified you.
Seek the LORD while he may be found,
    call upon him while he is near;
let the wicked forsake their way,
    and the unrighteous their thoughts;
let them return to the LORD, that he may have mercy
      on them,
    and to our God, for he will abundantly pardon.
For my thoughts are not your thoughts,
    nor are your ways my ways, says the LORD.

For as the heavens are higher than the earth,
    so are my ways higher than your ways
    and my thoughts than your thoughts.
For as the rain and the snow come down from heaven,
    and do not return there until they have watered the earth,
making it bring forth and sprout,
    giving seed to the sower and bread to the eater,
so shall my word be that goes out from my mouth;
    it shall not return to me empty,
but it shall accomplish that which I purpose,
    and succeed in the thing for which I sent it.
For you shall go out in joy,
    and be led back in peace;
the mountains and the hills before you
    shall burst into song,
    and all the trees of the field shall clap their hands.
Instead of the thorn shall come up the cypress;
    instead of the brier shall come up the myrtle;
and it shall be to the LORD for a memorial,
    for an everlasting sign that shall not be cut off.

A reading from the prophecy of Isaiah 12.3–6.

With joy you will draw water from the wells of salvation.
And you will say in that day:
    Give thanks to the LORD,
        call on his name;
    make known his deeds among the nations;
        proclaim that his name is exalted.
    Sing praises to the LORD, for he has done gloriously;
        let this be known in all the earth.
    Shout aloud and sing for joy, O royal Zion,
        for great in your midst is the Holy One of Israel.

Deacon: Wisdom!

Reader: The Lord is my illumination, and my Saviour, whom shall
I fear?
**The Lord is the defence of my life, of whom shall I be
afraid ?**

A reading from 1 Corinthians 10.1–4
I do not want you to be unaware, brothers and sisters, that our
ancestors were all under the cloud, and all passed through the sea,
and all were baptized into Moses in the cloud and in the sea, and all
ate the same spiritual food, and all drank the same spiritual drink.
For they drank from the spiritual rock that followed them, and the
rock was Christ.
Alleluia.
The voice of the Lord is upon the waters, the God of glory thunders,
the Lord is upon many waters.

A reading from the Gospel according to Mark 1.9–11
In those days Jesus came from Nazareth of Galilee and was baptized
by John in the Jordan. And just as he was coming up out of the
water, he saw the heavens torn apart and the Spirit descending like a
dove on him. And a voice came from heaven, 'You are my Son, the
Beloved; with you I am well pleased.'

Assistant minister or deacon: Let us pray to the Lord.
Lord, have mercy.

For the peace that is from above, and for the salvation of our souls:
for the peace of the whole world; for the welfare of God's holy
churches, and for the union of them all.
Let us pray to the Lord.
Lord, have mercy.

For our holy church, and for those who with faith, devoutness,
and in the fear of God have entered it, and for our bishop and
archbishops and for all the clergy and the laity, and for our most
God-fearing sovereign.
Let us pray to the Lord.
Lord, have mercy.

For this town, and for those who dwell therein.
Let us pray to the Lord.
Lord, have mercy.

For healthful seasons, for abundance of the fruits of the earth; and
for peaceful times.
Let us pray to the Lord.
Lord, have mercy.

For those who travel by sea or by land; for the sick and the suffering;
for those who are in captivity, and for their salvation.
Let us pray to the Lord.
Lord, have mercy.

That these waters may be sanctified by the power, and effectual operation, and inspiration of the Holy Spirit.
Let us pray to the Lord.
Lord, have mercy.

That there may descend upon these waters the cleansing operation of the supersubstantial Trinity.
Let us pray to the Lord.
Lord, have mercy.

That there may be bestowed upon them the grace of redemption, the blessing of Jordan, through the might, and operation, and descent of the Holy Spirit.
Let us pray to the Lord.
Lord, have mercy.

That Satan may speedily be crushed under our feet, and that every evil council directed against us may be brought to nought.
Let us pray to the Lord.
Lord, have mercy.

That the Lord our God will free us from every aspersion and temptation of the enemy, and make us worthy of the good things which he has promised.
Let us pray to the Lord.
Lord, have mercy.

That he will illumine us with the light of understanding and of piety, and with the inspiration of the Holy Spirit.
Let us pray to the Lord.
Lord, have mercy.

That the Lord our God will send down the blessing of Jordan and sanctify these waters.
Let us pray to the Lord.
Lord, have mercy.

That this water may be a gift of sanctification, a loosing of sins, for the healing of soul and body, and for every befitting need.
Let us pray to the Lord.
Lord, have mercy.

That this water may be a fountain welling forth unto life eternal.
Let us pray to the Lord.
Lord, have mercy.

That it may be manifested to the destruction of every counsel of visible and invisible enemies.
Let us pray to the Lord.
Lord, have mercy.

For those who shall draw of it and take of it for the sanctification of their homes.
Let us pray to the Lord.
Lord, have mercy.

That it may be to the cleansing of soul and body of all that with faith draw and partake of it.
Let us pray to the Lord.
Lord, have mercy.

That we may be counted worthy to be filled with sanctification through the partaking of these waters, by the invisible manifestation of the Holy Spirit.
Let us pray to the Lord.
Lord, have mercy.

That the Lord God may hearken unto the voice of the prayer of us sinners, and have mercy upon us.
Let us pray to the Lord.
Lord, have mercy.

That the Lord God will deliver us from all tribulation, wrath, peril and necessity.
Let us pray to the Lord.
Lord, have mercy.

Succour us, save us, have mercy upon us, and keep us, O God, by your grace.
Lord, have mercy.

Calling to remembrance our most holy, undefiled, most blessed and glorious Lady, the birth-giver of God and ever-virgin Mary, with all the saints, let us commend ourselves, and each other, and all our life to Christ our God.
To you, O Lord.

While the above prayers are said, it is traditional that the minister says the following prayer quietly.

O Lord Jesus Christ, the only-begotten Son, who is in the bosom of the Father, O true God, fountain of life and immortality, light of light, who came into the world to illuminate it, enlighten our minds with your Holy Spirit, and accept us who offer you majesty and thanksgiving for your marvellous and mighty works, which are from all eternity; and for your saving providence in these last ages, in which you have assumed our impotent and poor substance, and, condescending to the state of a servant, you who are king of all things did furthermore endure to be baptized in the River Jordan by the hand of a servant, that you, the sinless one, having sanctified the nature of water, might lead us unto regeneration by water and the Spirit, and establish us in the deliverance then first instituted for us. Celebrating the memory of this divine mystery, we beseech you, O Lord who loves humankind, sprinkle us, your unworthy servants, according to your divine promise, with pure water, the gift of your tenderness of heart, that the prayer of us sinners over this water may be acceptable through your grace, and that thereby your blessing may be bestowed upon us and upon all your faithful people, to the glory of your holy and adorable name. For to you is due all glory, honour and worship, with your Father who is from everlasting, and with your most holy, good and life-giving Spirit, now and forever, and to the ages of ages. Amen.

The minister traditionally then says the following prayer out loud.

Great you are, O Lord, and wonderful are your works, and no word shall be sufficient for the praise of your wonders. (*Said three times*)

For you by your will have from nothingness brought all things into being, and by your power you sustain creation, and by your providence you direct the world. When you had framed the universe out of four elements, you did crown the circle of the year with four seasons. All the reason-endowed powers tremble before you. The sun sings your praises, and the moon glorifies you; the stars, also, stand before your presence. The light obeys you. The depths shudder with awe before you; the springs of water do your bidding. You have spread out the heavens like a curtain, you have established the earth upon the waters, and have walled in the sea with sand. You have diffused the air for breathing. The angelic powers serve you. The choirs of angels worship you. The many-eyed cherubim and the six-winged seraphim, standing and flying around, cover themselves with awe before your unapproachable glory. For you, God who cannot be circumscribed, unbeginning and ineffable, came down upon earth, taking the form of a servant, and being made in the likeness of a man. For you could not endure, O Master, because of your tender-hearted mercy, to behold the human race tormented by the devil; but you came, and saved us. We confess your grace; we proclaim your mercy; we conceal not your beneficence. You have set at liberty the generations of our race; by your birth you have sanctified a virgin's womb. All creation sings praises to you who revealed yourself; for you are our God, who has been seen on earth, and dwelt among us. You hallowed, also, the streams of Jordan, sending down from heaven your Holy Spirit, and crushing the heads of the serpents which lurked there.

The minister makes the sign of the cross three times over the water while saying the blessing:

Wherefore do you, O King who loves humanity, be present now through the inspiration of your Holy Spirit and sanctify this water. (*Said three times*)

And give it the grace of redemption, the blessing of the Jordan. Make it a fountain of immortality, a gift of sanctification, a remission of sins, a healing of infirmities, a destruction of demons, unapproachable by hostile powers, filled with angelic strength. And may it be for all those who draw it and partake of it for the purification of their souls and bodies, for the healing of their passions, for the sanctification of their houses, and for every befitting need. For you are our God, who through water and the Spirit renews our nature fallen through sin. For you are our God, who with water overwhelmed sin in the days of Noah. For you are our God who by the sea, through Moses, set free the Hebrew race from slavery to Pharaoh. For you are our God, who divided the rock in the wilderness, so that water gushed forth, and made streams well forth abundantly and satisfied your thirsty people. For you are our God, who by fire and water, through Elijah, set Israel free from the error of Baal.

And now, O Master, sanctify this water by your Holy Spirit. (*Said three times*)

And grant to all those who touch it, and partake of it, and are sprinkled with it, sanctification, healing, cleansing and blessing. Save, O Lord, and show mercy to the most holy governing church, and keep them in peace beneath your shelter. Subdue under them every foe and adversary; grant them all their petitions for salvation and eternal life; that by the elements, and by humans, and by angels, and with all things visible and invisible, they may magnify your most holy name, together with the Father, and the Holy Spirit, now, and ever, and to the ages of ages.
Amen.

Minister: Peace be with you.
           And with your spirit.

Deacon: Bow your heads to the Lord.
           To you, O Lord.

The minister bows their head and prays:

Incline your ear, O Lord, and hear us, you were graciously pleased
to receive baptism in the Jordan, and sanctified the waters. Bless us
all who, by the bowing of our necks, indicate our humility of mind;
and graciously grant that we may be filled with your sanctification,
through partaking of this water, and through sprinkling. And may it
be to us, O Lord, for the healing of our souls and bodies.

For you are our sanctification, and to you we ascribe glory,
and thanksgiving, and worship, with your Father, who is from
everlasting, and with your most holy, and good, and life-creating
Spirit, now and ever, and to the ages of ages.
Amen.

*The minister blesses the water in cross pattern while holding the
cross, then dips it perpendicularly in the water, elevates then lowers it,
saying (or singing):*

When in the Jordan you were baptized, O Lord, the worship of the
Trinity was made manifest. For the voice of the Father bore witness
to you, calling you his beloved Son, and the Spirit, in the form of a
dove, testified to the surety of that word. O Christ, who was made
manifest, and who enlightens the world, glory to you.

*The dipping and words above are repeated for a second and third
time. The minister then takes some sanctified water in a salver, and
turns to face the west. The minister holds the cross in one hand and
in the other an aspergillum (a holy water sprinkler) filled with the
water while the congregation come up and have a cross signed on
their forehead with the water. After this, the rubric suggests re-entry
to the main church if the ritual is conducted by the font.*

Let us praise in song, O you faithful, the greatness of God's favour to us. For, having become man because of our transgressions, for our purification is he purified in the Jordan, he alone being pure and uncorrupt, who sanctifies me and the waters, and crushes the heads of the serpents in the water. Wherefore, brothers and sisters, let us draw that water with joy; for the grace of the Spirit is invisibly imparted to those who draw on it with faith, by Christ our God, who also is the Saviour of our souls.

Blessed be the Name of the Lord, henceforth, and forevermore. (*Said or sung three times*)

Psalm 34

I will bless the LORD at all times;
   his praise shall continually be in my mouth.
My soul makes its boast in the LORD;
   let the humble hear and be glad.
O magnify the LORD with me,
   and let us exalt his name together.
I sought the LORD, and he answered me,
   and delivered me from all my fears.
Look to him, and be radiant;
   so your faces shall never be ashamed.
This poor soul cried, and was heard by the LORD,
   and was saved from every trouble.
The angel of the LORD encamps
   around those who fear him, and delivers them.
O taste and see that the LORD is good;
   happy are those who take refuge in him.
O fear the LORD, you his holy ones,
   for those who fear him have no want.
The young lions suffer want and hunger,
   but those who seek the LORD lack no good thing.
Come, O children, listen to me;
   I will teach you the fear of the LORD.
Which of you desires life,
   and covets many days to enjoy good?
Keep your tongue from evil,
   and your lips from speaking deceit.
Depart from evil, and do good;
   seek peace, and pursue it.

The eyes of the LORD are on the righteous,
and his ears are open to their cry.
The face of the LORD is against evildoers,
to cut off the remembrance of them from the earth.
When the righteous cry for help, the LORD hears,
and rescues them from all their troubles.
The LORD is near to the brokenhearted,
and saves the crushed in spirit.
Many are the afflictions of the righteous,
but the LORD rescues them from them all.
He keeps all their bones;
not one of them will be broken.
Evil brings death to the wicked,
and those who hate the righteous will be condemned.
The LORD redeems the life of his servants;
none of those who take refuge in him will be condemned.

The people are offered holy water to drink; separate vessels or bottles of clean water can be blessed alongside any natural body of water for this purpose. The people are also given a piece of antidoron, *which is a blessed but not consecrated bread.*

Benediction

May he who was graciously pleased to accept baptism from John, in the Jordan, for the sake of our salvation, Christ our very God, through the prayers of his most pure Mother, and of all the saints, have mercy upon us and save us; for he is gracious and loves humankind.

Blessing of the River from a Bridge

This liturgy is kindly provided by Southwark Cathedral, which holds an annual blessing of the River Thames from London Bridge in fellowship with the clergy from the church of St Magnus the Martyr on the opposite bank. It is held on the Sunday celebrating the Baptism of Christ in the River Jordan, usually the first Sunday of Epiphany in the church calendar.

This service stipulates that a wooden cross is thrown into the river. It might be more appropriate, particularly with a smaller stream, to substitute a cross made of twigs or woven from grass, or indeed a scattering of petals. A Brigid's Cross, woven from rushes or reeds and based on Celtic traditions about St Brigid of Kildare, would make a particularly pleasing connection to ancient landscape lore. Whatever form it takes, we would encourage that only local and entirely natural materials are used.

Blessing of the River

Minister: In the name of the Father and of the Son and of the
Holy Spirit.
All: **Amen.**
I will take you from the nations:
and gather you from all countries.
I will sprinkle clean water upon you:
and purify you from all uncleanness.
A new heart I will give you:
and put a new spirit within you.
You shall be my people:
and I shall be your God.
The Lord be with you
and also with you.

Reading: Jeremiah 17.7–8

All turn to face downstream

Reader: A reading from the prophet Jeremiah.
Blessed are those who trust in the LORD, whose trust is the
LORD. They shall be like a tree planted by water, sending
out its roots by the stream.
It shall not fear when heat comes, and its leaves shall stay
green;
in the year of drought it is not anxious, and it does not
cease to bear fruit.
This is the word of the Lord.
Thanks be to God.

Reading: Psalm 46

Led by another reader

Reader: The response to the psalm is:
The river makes glad the city of God.

God is our refuge and strength,
a very present help in trouble;
Therefore we will not fear, though the earth should change,
and though the mountains shake in the heart of the sea;
The river makes glad the city of God.

Though the waters roar and foam,
and though the mountains tremble with its tumult.
There is a river whose streams make glad the city of God,
the holy habitation of the Most High.
The river makes glad the city of God.

God is in the midst of the city;
it shall not be moved;
God will help it when the morning dawns.
The nations are in an uproar, the kingdoms totter,
he utters his voice, the earth melts.
The river makes glad the city of God.

Reading: Revelation 22.1–5

Reader: A reading from the book of the Revelation to St John. The angel showed me the river of the water of life, bright as crystal, flowing from the throne of God and of the Lamb through the middle of the street of the city. On either side of the river is the tree of life with its twelve kinds of fruit, producing its fruit each month; and the leaves of the tree are for the healing of the nations. Nothing accursed will be found there any more. But the throne of God and of the Lamb will be in it, and his servants will worship him; they will see his face, and his name will be on their foreheads. And there will be no more night; they need no light of lamp or sun, for the Lord God will be their light, and they will reign for ever and ever. This is the word of the Lord.
Thanks be to God.

The Song of Ephrem the Syrian

Minister: Jesus, how wonderful your footsteps, walking on the waters!
You subdued the great sea beneath your feet.
**Yet to a little stream you subjected your head,
bending down to be baptized in it.**
The stream was like John who performed the baptism in it,
in their smallness each an image of the other.
**To the stream so little, to the servant so weak,
the Lord of them both subjected himself.**

Gospel reading: Mark 1.9–11

Reader: Hear the Gospel of our Lord Jesus Christ according to Mark.
Glory to you, O Lord.

In those days Jesus came from Nazareth of Galilee and was baptized by John in the Jordan. And just as he was coming up out of the water, he saw the heavens torn apart and the Spirit descending like a dove on him. And a voice came from heaven, 'You are my Son, the Beloved; with you I am well pleased.'
This is the Gospel of the Lord.
Praise to you, O Christ.

Prayers are offered for all those in the local community involved with the life of the river

The response is

> Lord, in your mercy:
> **hear our prayer.**

The Blessing of the River

Minister: The Lord be with you.
And also with you.
Lift up your hearts.
We lift them to the Lord.
Let us give thanks to the Lord our God.
It is right to give thanks and praise.
It is indeed right, it is our duty and our joy, at all times to
give you thanks and praise,
for today the grace of the Holy Spirit
in the form of a dove descended upon the waters.
Today the sun that never sets has risen
and the world is filled with splendour
by the light of the Lord.
Today the clouds drop down upon all people
the dew of righteousness from on high.
Today the Uncreated of his own will
accepts the laying on of hands from his own creature.
Today the waters of the Jordan
are transformed for healing by the coming of the Lord.
Today the blinding mist of the world is dispersed
by the Epiphany of our God.
Today things above keep feast with things below,
and things below commune with things above.
So, Father, accept our sacrifice of praise;
by the power of your life-giving Spirit
bless the waters of this great river
through your anointed Son, Jesus Christ our Lord,
to whom with you and the Holy Spirit
we lift our voices of praise:
**blessed be God, our strength and our salvation,
now and for ever.
Amen.**

At this point a woven cross is dropped in the water, or petals scattered

May your Holy Spirit, who has brought us to new birth in the family of your church, raise us in Christ, our anointed Lord, to full and eternal life. For all might, majesty and dominion are yours, now and for ever.
Alleluia! Amen.

The people are sprinkled with blessed water

God, who in Christ gives us a spring of water welling up to eternal life, perfect in you the image of his glory; and the blessing of God Almighty, the Father, the Son and the Holy Spirit be upon you and remain with you always.
Amen.

Let us go, rejoicing in the peace of Christ.
Thanks be to God.

Blessing of the Waters: The Syrian Ritual

This text is taken from a tenth- or eleventh-century Syrian manuscript held in the British Museum. It is thought to be a transcription of an order of service prepared by Jacob, bishop of Edessa, a prolific scholar of the early church who died in AD 708. Liturgies arising from Eastern traditions are not exactly famed for their brevity, but this one has particular merit in providing numerous short readings from the Bible, allowing a greater degree of participation by the outdoor congregation.

As the rubric makes clear, this is presented as an outdoor liturgy, taking place beside a river or well, an important example of directing liturgical action towards the environment. It is included for its rich evocation of biblical waters, from the first verses of Genesis onwards. The power of the landscape to harbour spiritual forces and energy, including a river dragon and the notion that a noxious body of water could be 'evil', has been left in place to illustrate how deeply the cosmos can be regarded as alive to Christian ritual.

The British Museum also holds a shorter manuscript version of another Syrian Epiphany water blessing, which is designed solely for use inside the church building and takes place on the evening before the festival, known as a lesser blessing service. The translation reproduced here was published in 1901 as part of a collection of early water blessing rituals, which also includes this other lesser blessing liturgy.[46]

Health and safety rules being what they were in eighth-century Syria, it is not advisable to copy the original suggestion that water drawn from the river or well is used in further rituals such as sprinkling on the congregation. For this we suggest that a separate vessel of clean water can be placed on the ground and blessed in a single action alongside the natural body of water.

The Syrian Epiphany Water Ritual

Psalm 71

We begin with the responsorial psalm for Epiphany, the minister and people alternating verses (Ps. 71:1–2, 7–8, 10–11, 12–13):

Minister: In you, O LORD, I take refuge;
let me never be put to shame.

All: **In your righteousness deliver me and rescue me;
incline your ear to me and save me.**

I have been like a portent to many,
but you are my strong refuge.
My mouth is filled with your praise,
and with your glory all day long.
For my enemies speak concerning me,
and those who watch for my life consult together.
They say, 'Pursue and seize that person
whom God has forsaken,
for there is no one to deliver.'
O God, do not be far from me;
O my God, make haste to help me!
Let my accusers be put to shame and consumed;
let those who seek to hurt me
be covered with scorn and disgrace.

Psalm 77.16

When the waters saw you, O God,
when the waters saw you, they were afraid;
the very deep trembled.

The liturgy then continues with a number of water-themed readings
from the Bible. Those reproduced here could therefore be substituted
with or supplemented by the following: the return of the remnant of
Israel and Judah from Isaiah 11.11–12.6, the miraculous restoration
of a well by Elisha in 2 Kings 2.19–22, the apostle St Philip baptizing
the Ethiopian eunuch in Acts 8.26–39, or a reading on cleansing and
the Holy Spirit from Hebrews 10.15–25.

A reading from Exodus 15.22–25

Then Moses ordered Israel to set out from the Red Sea, and they went
into the wilderness of Shur. They went three days in the wilderness and
found no water. When they came to Marah, they could not drink the
water of Marah because it was bitter. That is why it was called Marah.
And the people complained against Moses, saying, 'What shall we
drink?' He cried out to the LORD; and the LORD showed him a piece of
wood; he threw it into the water, and the water became sweet. There
the LORD made for them a statute and an ordinance.
When the waters saw you, O God,
when the waters saw you, they were afraid;
the very deep trembled.

A reading from the book of Ezekiel 47.1–12

Then he brought me back to the entrance of the temple; there, water was flowing from below the threshold of the temple toward the east (for the temple faced east); and the water was flowing down from below the south end of the threshold of the temple, south of the altar. Then he brought me out by way of the north gate, and led me around on the outside to the outer gate that faces toward the east; and the water was coming out on the south side.

Going on eastward with a cord in his hand, the man measured one thousand cubits, and then led me through the water; and it was ankle-deep. Again he measured one thousand, and led me through the water; and it was knee-deep. Again he measured one thousand, and led me through the water; and it was up to the waist. Again he measured one thousand, and it was a river that I could not cross, for the water had risen; it was deep enough to swim in, a river that could not be crossed. He said to me, 'Mortal, have you seen this?'

Then he led me back along the bank of the river. As I came back, I saw on the bank of the river a great many trees on the one side and on the other. He said to me, 'This water flows toward the eastern region and goes down into the Arabah; and when it enters the sea, the sea of stagnant waters, the water will become fresh. Wherever the river goes, every living creature that swarms will live, and there will be very many fish, once these waters reach there. It will become fresh; and everything will live where the river goes. People will stand fishing beside the sea from En-gedi to En-eglaim; it will be a place for the spreading of nets; its fish will be of a great many kinds, like the fish of the Great Sea. But its swamps and marshes will not become fresh; they are to be left for salt. On the banks, on both sides of the river, there will grow all kinds of trees for food. Their leaves will not wither nor their fruit fail, but they will bear fresh fruit every month, because the water for them flows from the sanctuary. Their fruit will be for food, and their leaves for healing.'

When the waters saw you, O God,
when the waters saw you, they were afraid;
the very deep trembled.

A reading from the Gospel according to John 4.5–24

So he came to a Samaritan city called Sychar, near the plot of ground that Jacob had given to his son Joseph. Jacob's well was there, and Jesus, tired out by his journey, was sitting by the well. It was about noon.

A Samaritan woman came to draw water, and Jesus said to her, 'Give me a drink.' (His disciples had gone to the city to buy food.) The Samaritan woman said to him, 'How is it that you, a Jew, ask a drink of me, a woman of Samaria?' (Jews do not share things in common with Samaritans.) Jesus answered her, 'If you knew the gift of God, and who it is that is saying to you, "Give me a drink," you would have asked him, and he would have given you living water.' The woman said to him, 'Sir, you have no bucket, and the well is deep. Where do you get that living water? Are you greater than our ancestor Jacob, who gave us the well, and with his sons and his flocks drank from it?' Jesus said to her, 'Everyone who drinks of this water will be thirsty again, but those who drink of the water that I will give them will never be thirsty. The water that I will give will become in them a spring of water gushing up to eternal life.' The woman said to him, 'Sir, give me this water, so that I may never be thirsty or have to keep coming here to draw water.'

Jesus said to her, 'Go, call your husband, and come back.' The woman answered him, 'I have no husband.' Jesus said to her, 'You are right in saying, "I have no husband"; for you have had five husbands, and the one you have now is not your husband. What you have said is true!' The woman said to him, 'Sir, I see that you are a prophet. Our ancestors worshipped on this mountain, but you say that the place where people must worship is in Jerusalem.' Jesus said to her, 'Woman, believe me, the hour is coming when you will worship the Father neither on this mountain nor in Jerusalem. You worship what you do not know; we worship what we know, for salvation is from the Jews. But the hour is coming, and is now here, when the true worshippers will worship the Father in spirit and truth, for the Father seeks such as these to worship him. God is spirit, and those who worship him must worship in spirit and truth.'
When the waters saw you, O God,
when the waters saw you, they were afraid;
the very deep trembled.

Epiphany canticle (Rev. 4.11; 5.9b–10)

'You are worthy, our Lord and God,
to receive glory and honour and power,
for you created all things,
and by your will they existed and were created.
You are worthy to take the scroll
and to open its seals,

for you were slaughtered and by your blood you ransomed for God
saints from every tribe and language and people and nation;
you have made them to be a kingdom and priests serving our God,
and they will reign on earth.'
To the One who sits on the throne and to the Lamb
be blessing and honour, glory and might,
for ever and ever. Amen.

Let us all bow our heads in fear before the Lord.
Before you, O Lord, our God.

*At this point the deacons or assistants are instructed to fan the
waters, a ritual symbolism calling to mind the Spirit breathing over
the waters of chaos at the start of creation*

Glory be to God, and to the Son, and to the Holy Spirit, now and
always, and for ever and ever. Amen.
Amen.

O Lord God of our ancestors, who by the hand of your servant
Moses changed through the mystery of the wood of the cross bitter
waters into sweet, and gave your people who were thirsty water
to drink; and healed the evil, and barren, and unfruitful waters
by means of salt, which could be perceived by its taste, thereby
prefiguring the heavenly salt, by the hand of Elisha the Prophet;
who in your ineffable wisdom changed the nature of the water into
that of wine; and sanctified the waters of the River Jordan; now by
spiritual and apostolic salt, and by your invisible power, and by your
abundant and ineffable mercy to all people, and by the inspiration
of your Holy and life-giving Spirit, who is co-equal with you in
existence and everlastingness, bless and sanctify these waters. And
grant that they may be for the health and healing of the soul, and
body, and spirit of all those who partake of them, and who make use
of them.

For you are a God who loves people, and you are merciful, and you
desire life and redemption for those you have chosen; for you are
rightfully and properly all glory, and honour, and dominion, you the
one holy and adorable Trinity, coequal in being, of Father, and Son,
and Holy Spirt, now and always and for ever and ever. Amen.
Amen.

Let us bow our heads.
Before you, O God.

The minister then bows for the following prayer

O Lord God, mighty one and sustainer of all things, you who in the celestial heights are secretly and in an incomprehensible manner praised and glorified by the hosts and congregations of beings endowed with reason; you by whose word the heavens were made, and by the breath of whose mouth all your hosts were created; you who look upon the earth and it trembles, who rebukes the sea and dries it up; now by the riches of your grace make us all worthy of your great and abundant mercy, in this hour, and in the day of your glorious Epiphany, being pleased to return upon us; change our earthly minds and our hearts into purity of understanding, and make us ready for the great festival of your Epiphany and to receive these holy waters which have been sanctified by grace and loving kindness, that they may be for us all for the propitiation of offences, and for the remission of sins, and for the sprinkling and purification from every evil intent. By your angelic hosts protect us until our last breath, in blameless conduct of life and in the straight, spotless, blessed and unchanging faith. And bestow on us all chaste lives which shall be pleasing to you, whereby we may become worthy of the blessings which have been promised to your saints who from olden time have pleased you, the prophets, apostles, martyrs, confessors, the just, the righteous, ascetics, preachers of the fear of God, and all those who have kept your commandments diligently, through whose holy prayers we who are helpless may be armed, and may become clothed in their boldness of speech. And we beseech and entreat your gracious mercy, which loves all people, to be mindful of the dangers and persecutions for your holy name's sake of your holy, catholic, and apostolic church from one end of the inhabited world to the other, and do away from it schisms, and contentions, and divisions, and all the destructive heresies which spring up through the agency of the false one. And remember the remnant of the orthodox, and forget not your covenant, for we have been brought exceedingly low, but help us, O God our redeemer, for the sake of your great and marvellous name by which we have been called, and make us all worthy so that with a pure and holy conscience we may lift up glory and praise ceaselessly to your holy, and co-equal, and uncreated, and everlasting Trinity.

Here the minister lifts up his or her voice

How great you are, O Lord, and how marvellous are your works; no word is sufficient to describe the glory of your wonders. For, having by your power brought everything into being from things which had no being, by your dominion do you support creation, and by your care do you direct and provide the world with food. You have fashioned creation out of four elements, and have crowned the course of the year with four seasons. The heavenly host of beings who are endowed with reason tremble before you, and the orders of angels praise you, and the companies of archangels bow down in homage before you, the six-winged Seraphim fly around you and cry out, singing praises to you, and the many-eyed Cherubim shroud you in glory which cannot be approached. The sun praises you; the moon glorifies you; the stars praise you; the light is obedient to you; the depths tremble before you, and the fountains of water serve you. You have spread out the heavens like a bow, you have beaten out the earth over the waters, you have shut in the sea with the sand, and you have poured out the air like a breath. And you, being God who is without beginning or end, who cannot be comprehended, came down to earth, and took the form of a servant, and lived in the form of a human child. For, O our Lord, by reason of your saving mercy, you could not bear to see the children of men and women oppressed by the evil one, but did come and deliver them. We confess your goodness, and we proclaim abroad your mercy, and we will not hide the fair beauty of that which you have done. You did bless the child of nature, and you did by your birth sanctify the virgin womb, and all creation praised you when you were revealed. For you, O our God, did appear upon the earth, and with the children of men and women did you live and move. You sanctified for us the waters of the Jordan when your Holy Spirit came from heaven and landed on them, and you broke the head of the dragon which writhed therein. O Lord, who loves all people, come now by the descent of your Holy Spirit and sanctify these waters. Give them the grace of Jordan, and make them to be fountains of blessings, and gifts of holiness, and a loosing of sins, and a binding up of sicknesses, and chasing away of devils, and things unapproachable by opposing hosts, and things filled with angelic power, so that to all those who draw from and partake of them they may be for the cleansing of souls and bodies, and the healing of passions, and the sanctification of houses, and ready to bring benefits of every kind. For you are the one who by water and the Spirit renewed our nature which had become old through sin. You are the one who by water did away the sin which was in the days of Noah. You are the one who by the sea set free the race of the Hebrews from the oppression of Pharaoh.

You are the one who by water and fire delivered Israel from the error of Baal by the hands of Elijah the Prophet. And now, O our Lord, while sanctifying these waters by your Holy Spirit, grant those who touch them, or who partake of them, or who make use of them in any way whatsoever in true faith, praise, and holiness, and blessing, and purification, and health, so that by the material elements of the world, and by the children of men and women, and by angels, and by things visible, and by things invisible, your name may be praised, together with your Father and your Holy Spirit now and always and for ever and ever. Amen.
Amen.

The minister signs three crosses over the surface of the waters, saying:

These waters are blessed in the name of the Father, the Living One, to life. Amen. And in the name of the Son, the Living One, to life. Amen. And in the name of the Living and Holy Spirit, to life, for ever and ever. Amen.
Amen.

The minister bows and says:

O creator of the waters, and maker of all things, who holds all things by the dominion of your majesty; who spoke and they came into being; who commands and the heavens, the earth, and all creatures were created; who by your will and by the ruling command of your operative power gave the command and out of nothing everything came into being and into the well-ordered and sure condition in which all things exist; you who makes and changes everything into good; now also we pray make and change these waters by the power of your Holy Spirit, and give them power and sanctify them by your gift against every opposing agency which might be stirred up or wrought through the purpose and intention of the evil one by means of sorcery, the art of magic, or astrology, or incantations; and grant that they may be to all those who take them in the faith of the truth, either for drinking or for any purpose whatsoever, happiness, and pleasantness, and a cleansing of the conscience; and a healing, and a refreshing, and for the health of both soul and body, through the bestowal of abundant mercy from you, through the grace and mercy and love for humanity of your only Son, our Lord and God and Redeemer, Jesus Christ, and of the Holy Spirit.

The minister raises his or her voice, saying:

O Lord of all things, creator of all which has been set in order, maker of all creation; you who has at all times made and prepared everything for the redemption and benefit of the whole human race; who by the hand of Moses made sweet the bitter waters by means of wood, and healed them for the quenching of the thirst of the people; you who made healthy the evil and barren waters of the brook by the hand of Elisha the prophet; you who changed the nature of the waters at Cana in Galilee into wine, and there showed yourself to be the Lord and creator of creation; now also O Lord, lover of all people, by the inspiration of your grace bless and sanctify these waters so that they may be to all who partake of them a cause of gratitude and perfect redemption, and of turning aside from every evil act, and for the enjoyment of a peaceful mind which is from you, for you are the blessed God who loves humanity, and to you with your Father and your Holy Spirit are due all honour and glory and dominion now, and always and for ever. Amen.
Amen.

Holy are you, O God.
Holy are you, O God.

The minister picks up a vessel with water that has been sanctified; if the water is to be used for any further rituals such as sprinkling then clean and fresh water, rather than water drawn from the river or well, will need to be used. Holding the vessel in his or her right hand, the minister says the following prayer:

O creator of the waters, O maker of all things who makes and changes everything, make and change these waters by the power of your Holy Spirit, and strengthen them against every opposing agency, and grant that they may be to all of those who make use of them for drinking, or for washing, or for sprinkling, or for any other purpose whatsoever, for the healing of both soul and body, and for bountiful mercy which is from you, and for keeping all of us away from evil, and for the redemption, peace and sanctification of our lives in Christ Jesus our Lord, to whom with you and your most Holy Spirit all glory and honour and dominion are due, now and always and for ever. Amen.
Amen.

After this the water can be distributed for sprinkling, for blessing in homes, or taken back to church for further ritual use

Sea Sunday Service and Blessing of Boats

Seafarers of every kind have reason to be thankful for the sea, not least at Dartmouth in Devon, a community built around a safe natural harbour at the mouth of the River Dart where boating and fishing remain the lifeblood of many. Water has a special  resonance when it comes to arriving or leaving, since three passenger and car ferries remain the only way to cross the estuary. Dartmouth has no physical bridges, but makes up for the lack with a strong spiritual connection between the land and the sea, one that finds full expression in two services held on Sea Sunday by the local parish church of St Clement's and its united benefice.

The first service is a blessing of the boats that involves up to 30 vessels, including fishing, naval and of course the RNLI lifeboat charity. In Dartmouth, the priest steps between each boat, strikingly clad in both robes and a lifejacket, to bless each individual craft, before returning safely to the town pontoon where the community is gathered. The second service is based on Evensong in the Book of Common Prayer, and is held at the united benefice's church of St Petrox at the mouth of the river. It includes a procession out of the church building to the bankside, where the river and sea are blessed. A sea blessing service could be conducted entirely outdoors.

St Clement is a particularly resonant patron saint for a coastal church, often depicted with the anchor that was used in his martyrdom in the Black Sea in the year AD 99. He was Pope at the time of his execution, and has been honoured ever since as patron saint of mariners. Sea Sunday is celebrated on the second Sunday in July.

Collections are taken for The Mission to Seafarers, an Anglican Christian charity which operates around the world through a network of chaplains.[47] The two services below are reproduced by kind permission of the vicar and churchwardens of the United Benefice of Dartmouth and Dittisham. The language has been very slightly modernized, and the blessing elements of both services could easily be adapted for use in more traditional, more modern, or alternative settings.

1 *Sea Sunday Service and Blessing of Boats*

Minister: We gather in the name of Jesus Christ who calmed the storm, the one whom even the wind and the waves obey. The Lord be with you

All: **And also with you.**

Introduction

Hymn

The suggested hymn is 'Will your anchor hold in the storms of life'

Opening prayer

Let us pray.
Almighty Father creator of the oceans and land
Whose Son sailed the seas and calmed the storms.
Anoint all seafarers with your Holy Spirit,
That as it breathed over the waters of creation,
So may you bring newness of life to them and us.
Through Jesus Christ our Lord.
Amen

Bible reading: Acts 27.39–28.2

Reader: A reading from the Acts of the Apostles.
In the morning they did not recognize the land, but they noticed a bay with a beach, on which they planned to run the ship ashore, if they could. So they cast off the anchors and left them in the sea. At the same time they loosened the ropes that tied the steering-oars; then hoisting the foresail to the wind, they made for the beach. But striking a reef, they ran the ship aground; the bow stuck and remained immovable, but the stern was being broken up by the force of the waves. The soldiers' plan was to kill the prisoners, so that none might swim away and escape; but the centurion, wishing to save Paul, kept them from carrying out their plan. He ordered those who could swim to jump overboard first and make for the land, and the rest to follow, some on planks and others on pieces of the ship. And so it was that all were brought safely to land. After we had reached safety, we then learned that the island was

called Malta. The natives showed us unusual kindness.
Since it had begun to rain and was cold, they kindled a fire
and welcomed all of us around it.
This is the word of the Lord.
Thanks be to God.

Hymn or song

Gospel reading: John 21.1–6

Reader: A reading from the Gospel according to John.
After these things Jesus showed himself again to the
disciples by the Sea of Tiberias; and he showed himself
in this way. Gathered there together were Simon Peter,
Thomas called the Twin, Nathanael of Cana in Galilee,
the sons of Zebedee, and two others of his disciples. Simon
Peter said to them, 'I am going fishing.' They said to him,
'We will go with you.' They went out and got into the
boat, but that night they caught nothing.

Just after daybreak, Jesus stood on the beach; but the
disciples did not know that it was Jesus. Jesus said to
them, 'Children, you have no fish, have you?' They
answered him, 'No.' He said to them, 'Cast the net to the
right side of the boat, and you will find some.' So they cast
it, and now they were not able to haul it in because there
were so many fish.
This is the Gospel of the Lord.
Thanks be to God.

Prayers

After each prayer the reader will say:

Lord, in your mercy
hear our prayer.

The Lord's Prayer

As our Saviour taught us, so we pray
Our Father …

Blessing of boats

The minister then steps between the boats and blesses them individually with holy water. A minister who is a priest or deacon says the prayer of blessing with hands outstretched; a lay minister says the prayer with hands joined.

God of boundless love,
at the beginning of creation
your Spirit hovered over the deep.
You called forth every creature,
and the seas teemed with life.
Through your Son Jesus Christ,
you have given us the rich harvest of salvation.
Bless this gig, its equipment and all who will use it.
Protect them from the dangers of wind and rain
and all the perils of the deep.
May Christ, who calmed the storm
and filled the nets of his disciples,
bring us all to the harbour of light and peace.
Grant this through Christ our Lord.
Amen.

Final prayer, to which all respond

Amen.

Hymn

Suggested hymn: 'Lead us, heavenly Father, lead us'

Final blessing

Minister: The Lord be with you
and also with you.

The peace of God which passes all understanding
keep your hearts and minds in the knowledge and love
of God,
and of His Son, Jesus Christ our Lord.
And may the blessing of God almighty,
the Father, and the Son, and the Holy Spirit
be upon you, and remain with you always.
Amen.

2 *Choral Evensong for Sea Sunday*

Welcome

A welcome is given, concluding with the words:

> Today we pray for all who go down to the sea in ships and
> we give thanks for the place of the river and the sea in the
> life of this wonderful place.

Introit

*The following introit is sung, 'Save me O God, from waves that
roll', using the version of music composed by the nineteenth-century
Dartmouth musician Stephen Jarvis. Alternatively some or all of
Psalm 69 could be recited antiphonally.*

Processional hymn

> *The suggested hymn is* 'Amazing grace! How sweet the sound'

Minister: O Lord, open thou our lips
All: **and our mouth shall show forth thy praise.**
           O God, make speed to save us.
           O Lord, make haste to help us.
           Glory be to the Father, and to the Son, and to the
           Holy Ghost;
           **as it was in the beginning, is now, and ever shall be, world
           without end. Amen.**
           Praise ye the Lord.
           The Lord's name be praised.

Psalm 107.23–32

> Some went down to the sea in ships,
> doing business on the mighty waters;
> **they saw the deeds of the LORD,**
> **his wondrous works in the deep.**
> For he commanded and raised the stormy wind,
> which lifted up the waves of the sea.
> **They mounted up to heaven, they went down to the depths;**
> **their courage melted away in their calamity;**
> they reeled and staggered like drunkards,
> and were at their wits' end.

Then they cried to the LORD in their trouble,
and he brought them out from their distress;
he made the storm be still,
and the waves of the sea were hushed.
Then they were glad because they had quiet,
and he brought them to their desired haven.
Let them thank the LORD for his steadfast love,
for his wonderful works to humankind.
Let them extol him in the congregation of the people,
and praise him in the assembly of the elders.
Glory be to the Father, and to the Son, and to the Holy
Ghost; as it was in the beginning, is now, and ever shall
be, world without end. Amen.

First reading

Reader: A reading from the book of Genesis, chapter 7.
Then the LORD said to Noah, 'Go into the ark, you and
all your household, for I have seen that you alone are
righteous before me in this generation. Take with you
seven pairs of all clean animals, the male and its mate; and
a pair of the animals that are not clean, the male and its
mate; and seven pairs of the birds of the air also, male and
female, to keep their kind alive on the face of all the earth.
For in seven days I will send rain on the earth for forty
days and forty nights; and every living thing that I have
made I will blot out from the face of the ground.' And
Noah did all that the LORD had commanded him.

Noah was six hundred years old when the flood of waters
came on the earth. And Noah with his sons and his wife
and his sons' wives went into the ark to escape the waters
of the flood. Of clean animals, and of animals that are
not clean, and of birds, and of everything that creeps on
the ground, two and two, male and female, went into the
ark with Noah, as God had commanded Noah. And after
seven days the waters of the flood came on the earth.

In the six-hundredth year of Noah's life, in the second
month, on the seventeenth day of the month, on that day
all the fountains of the great deep burst forth, and the
windows of the heavens were opened. The rain fell on
the earth forty days and forty nights. On the very same

day Noah with his sons, Shem and Ham and Japheth, and Noah's wife and the three wives of his sons entered the ark, they and every wild animal of every kind, and all domestic animals of every kind, and every creeping thing that creeps on the earth, and every bird of every kind – every bird, every winged creature. They went into the ark with Noah, two and two of all flesh in which there was the breath of life. And those that entered, male and female of all flesh, went in as God had commanded him; and the LORD shut him in.

The flood continued forty days on the earth; and the waters increased, and bore up the ark, and it rose high above the earth. The waters swelled and increased greatly on the earth; and the ark floated on the face of the waters. The waters swelled so mightily on the earth that all the high mountains under the whole heaven were covered; the waters swelled above the mountains, covering them fifteen cubits deep. And all flesh died that moved on the earth, birds, domestic animals, wild animals, all swarming creatures that swarm on the earth, and all human beings; everything on dry land in whose nostrils was the breath of life died. He blotted out every living thing that was on the face of the ground, human beings and animals and creeping things and birds of the air; they were blotted out from the earth. Only Noah was left, and those that were with him in the ark. And the waters swelled on the earth for one hundred and fifty days.

Magnificat

To be said or sung by the whole congregation

> Tell out, my soul, the greatness of the Lord
> Unnumbered blessings, give my spirit voice;
> Tender to me the promise of his word;
> In God my Saviour shall my heart rejoice.
>
> Tell out, my soul, the greatness of his name:
> make known his might, the deeds his arm has done;
> His mercy sure, from age to age the same;
> His holy name, the Lord, the mighty one.

Tell out, my soul, the greatness of his might:
Pow'rs and dominions lay their glory by;
Proud hearts and stubborn wills are put to flight,
The hungry fed, the humble lifted high.

Tell out, my soul, the glories of his word:
Firm is his promise, and his mercy sure.
Tell out, my soul, the greatness of the Lord
To children's children and for evermore.

Second reading

Reader: A reading from the Gospel according to John 21.1–12.
After these things Jesus showed himself again to the
disciples by the Sea of Tiberias; and he showed himself
in this way. Gathered there together were Simon Peter,
Thomas called the Twin, Nathanael of Cana in Galilee,
the sons of Zebedee, and two others of his disciples. Simon
Peter said to them, 'I am going fishing.' They said to him,
'We will go with you.' They went out and got into the
boat, but that night they caught nothing.

Just after daybreak, Jesus stood on the beach; but the
disciples did not know that it was Jesus. Jesus said to
them, 'Children, you have no fish, have you?' They
answered him, 'No.' He said to them, 'Cast the net to the
right side of the boat, and you will find some.' So they cast
it, and now they were not able to haul it in because there
were so many fish. That disciple whom Jesus loved said
to Peter, 'It is the Lord!' When Simon Peter heard that it
was the Lord, he put on some clothes, for he was naked,
and jumped into the sea. But the other disciples came in
the boat, dragging the net full of fish, for they were not far
from the land, only about a hundred yards off.

When they had gone ashore, they saw a charcoal fire there,
with fish on it, and bread. Jesus said to them, 'Bring some
of the fish that you have just caught.' So Simon Peter
went aboard and hauled the net ashore, full of large fish,
a hundred fifty-three of them; and though there were so
many, the net was not torn. Jesus said to them, 'Come and
have breakfast.' Now none of the disciples dared to ask
him, 'Who are you?' because they knew it was the Lord.

Nunc Dimittis

Faithful vigil ended,
watching, waiting cease;
Master, grant thy servant
his discharge in peace.
All thy Spirit promised,
all the Father willed;
Now these eyes behold it
perfectly fulfilled.
This thy great deliverance
sets thy people free;
Christ, their light uplifted
all the nations see.
Christ, thy people's glory!
Watching, doubting, cease;
Grant to us thy servants
our discharge in peace.

The Apostles' Creed

I believe in God the Father almighty, maker of heaven and earth: and
in Jesus Christ his only Son our Lord, who was conceived by the Holy
Ghost, born of the Virgin Mary, suffered under Pontius Pilate, was
crucified, dead, and buried. He descended into hell; the third day he
rose again from the dead; he ascended into heaven, and sitteth on the
right hand of God the Father almighty; from thence he shall come to
judge the quick and the dead. I believe in the Holy Ghost; the holy
Catholick Church; the communion of saints; the forgiveness of sins;
the resurrection of the body, and the life everlasting. Amen.

The Lord be with you.
And with thy spirit.

Let us pray.
Lord, have mercy upon us.
Christ, have mercy upon us.

Lord, have mercy upon us.
Our Father,
which art in heaven, hallowed be thy name; thy kingdom come; thy
will be done, in earth as it is in heaven. Give us this day our daily
bread. And forgive us our trespasses, as we forgive them that trespass

against us. **And lead us not into temptation; but deliver us from evil. Amen.**

O Lord, show thy mercy upon us.
And grant us thy salvation.
O Lord, save the Queen.
And mercifully hear us when we call upon thee.
Endue thy ministers with righteousness.
And make thy chosen people joyful.
O Lord, save thy people.
And bless thine inheritance.
Give peace in our time, O Lord.
Because there is none other that fighteth for us,
but only thou, O God.
O God, make clean our hearts within us.
And take not thy Holy Spirit from us.

Collect for Sea Sunday

Lord God, creator of land and sea, bless those who work at sea. Be with them in fair weather and foul, in danger or distress. Strengthen them when weary, lift them up when down and comfort them when far from their loved ones. In this life, bring them safely to shore and, in the life to come, welcome them to your kingdom. For Jesus Christ's sake.
Amen.

Collect for Peace

O God, from whom all holy desires, all good counsels, and all just works do proceed; give unto thy servants that peace which the world cannot give; that our hearts may be set to obey thy commandments, and also that by thee, we, being defended from the fear of our enemies may pass our time in rest and quietness; through the merits of Jesus Christ our Saviour.
Amen.

Collect for Aid Against All Perils

Lighten our darkness, we beseech thee, O Lord; and by thy great mercy defend us from all perils and dangers of this night; for the love of thy only Son, our Saviour, Jesus Christ.
Amen.

Anthem

The suggested anthem is 'They that go down to the sea in ships' *(words from Psalm 107, music by Herbert Sumsion, former organist of Gloucester Cathedral)*

Prayers

Prayers are led for the church, for the world and for all those in need. The prayers conclude with the Grace.

The grace of our Lord Jesus Christ, and the love of God, and the fellowship of the Holy Ghost, be with us all evermore. Amen.

Hymn

The suggested hymn is 'Thou whose almighty word', *during which a collection can be taken to support the work of charities such as the Mission to Seafarers*

Sermon

Hymn

The suggested hymn is 'Eternal Father, strong to save'; *during the service in Dartmouth this is the point where the congregation process out of the church to the riverside*

Blessing of the Waters

Minister: You fountains of waters bless the Lord.
All: **All you seas and waves bless the Lord.**
Our help is in the name of the Lord.
Who made heaven and earth.
Lord, heed my prayer.
And let my cry be heard by you.
The Lord be with you.
And also with you.

Prayer of Blessing

Let us pray.
Almighty and everlasting God, Father of incomprehensible majesty, whose invisible power can be glimpsed from your visible creation; O God, whose Spirit hovered over the waters in the beginning of the

world, grant to us, your servants, that as often as we behold with our bodily eyes the mighty waters swelling out in billows on the heavenly horizon, we may be enraptured in contemplation of your hidden mysteries. Let such a sight and the thoughts it arouses prompt us to invoke and to glorify with due praise your holy name, and to render to you, to whose empire all creatures are subject, the homage of our minds in true humility and devotion; through Christ our Lord.
Amen.

Lord Jesus Christ, who once walked upon the waters, who uttered a word of command to the raging tempest of wind and sea and there came a great calm; let your piteous glance fall upon us, your servants, who find themselves surrounded by the many perils of this life; and grant that by the power of your blessing + poured out on these waters all wicked spirits may be repelled, the danger of the tempestuous winds may subside, and that all who are voyaging on the seas may safely reach their destination, and finally return unharmed to their homes. We ask this of you who lives and reigns forever and ever.
Amen.

Lord, who said, 'In the sweat of your brow you shall eat your bread'; kindly heed our prayers and bestow your blessing + on this sea, so that all who are obliged to earn their daily bread for themselves and their families by traversing these waters may be enriched with your bounty and offer you due gratitude for your goodness; through Christ our Lord.
Amen.

The minister then sprinkles the waters with holy water

Blessing

Bless, O Lord, all who sail in ships. Preserve them for yourself. Bless all who service them, and lead us all into your kingdom; through Christ our Lord.
Amen.

The peace of God, which passes all understanding, keep your hearts and minds in the knowledge and love of God, and of his Son Jesus Christ our Lord: And the blessing of God Almighty, the Father, the Son, and the Holy Ghost, be amongst you and remain with you always.
Amen.

Go in the peace of Christ
Thanks be to God.

Sea and Ocean Blessings
from the *Carmina Gadelica*

These three blessings speak of communities closely bound up with life on the sea, reflecting the coastal communities of western Scotland where they originate. All three were printed in the *Carmina Gadelica*, the compilation of oral traditions, prayers and local lore gathered, translated and edited by the folklorist Alexander Carmichael during the late nineteenth century.[48]

They are described as two ocean blessings and a sea blessing, and indeed all three are similar prayers for propitious weather and waves during a journey. The sea blessing appears to be composed for recitation when in dock, before embarking on a journey, because it has a responsorial formula that requires the participation of the crew and then the participation of 'all', presumably referring to an on-shore congregation.

1 The Ocean Blessing

O thou who pervadest the heights,
Imprint on us thy gracious blessing,
Carry us over the surface of the sea,
Carry us safely to a haven of peace,
Bless our boatmen and our boat,
Bless our anchors and our oars,
Each stay and halyard and traveller,
Our mainsails to our tall masts.
Keep, O king of the elements, in their place
That we may return home in peace;
I myself will sit down at the helm,
It is God's own Son who will give me guidance,
As he gave to Columba the mild
What time he set stay to sails.

Mary, Bride,[49] Michael, Paul,
Peter, Gabriel, John of love,
Pour ye down the dew from above
That would make our faith to grow.
Establish ye us in the Rock of rocks,
In every law that love exhibits,
That we may reach the land of glory,
Where peace and love and mercy reign,
All vouchsafed to us through grace;
Never shall the canker worm get near us,
We shall be safe there for ever,
We shall not be in the bonds of death
Though we are of the seed of Adam.

On the Feast Day of Michael, the Feast Day of Martin,
The Feast Day of Andrew, band of mercy,
The Feast Day of Bride, day of my choice,
Cast ye the serpent into the ocean,
So that the sea may swallow her up;
On the Feast Day of Patrick, day of power,
Foreshow to us the storm from the north,
Quell its wrath and blunt its fury,
Lessen its fierceness, kill its cold.

On the day of the Three Kings on high,
Subdue to us the crest of the waves,
On Beltane Day give us the dew,
On John's Day the gentle wind,
The Day of Mary the great of fame,
Ward off us the storm from the west;
Each day and night, storm and calm,
Be thou with us, O Chief of chiefs,
Be thou thyself to us a compass-chart,
Be thine hand on the helm of our rudder,
Thine own hand, thou God of the elements,
Early and late as is becoming,
Early and late as is becoming.

2 *Ocean Blessing*

God the Father all-powerful, benign,
Jesu the Son of tears and of sorrow,
With thy co-assistance, O! Holy Spirit.

The Three-One, ever-living, ever-mighty, everlasting,
Who brought the children of Israel through the Red Sea,
And Jonah to land from the belly of the great creature of the ocean,

Who brought Paul and his companions in the ship,
From the torment of the sea, from the dolour of the waves,
From the gale that was great, from the storm that was heavy.

Sain us and shield and sanctify us,
Be thou, King of the elements, seated at our helm,
And lead us in peace to the end of our journey.

With winds mild, kindly, benign, pleasant,
Without swirl, without whirl, without eddy,
That would do no harmful deed to us.

We ask all things of thee, O God,
According to thine own will and word.

3 Sea Prayer

Captain: Blest be the boat.
(or minister)

Crew: **God the Father bless her.**
           Blest be the boat.
           God the Son bless her.
           Blest be the boat.
           God the Spirit bless her.

All: **God the Father,**
           God the Son,
           God the Spirit,
           Bless the boat.

Minister: What can befall you
           And God the Father with you?
Crew: **No harm can befall us.**
           What can befall you
           And God the Son with you?
           No harm can befall us.
           What can befall you
           And God the Spirit with you?
           No harm can befall us.

All: **God the Father,**
           God the Son,
           God the Spirit,
           With us eternally.

           What can cause you anxiety
           And the God of the elements over you?
Crew: **No anxiety can be ours.**
           What can cause you anxiety
           And the King of the elements over you?
           No anxiety can be ours.
           What can cause you anxiety
           And the Spirit of the elements over you?
           No anxiety can be ours.

All: **The God of the elements.**
           The King of the elements,
           The Spirit of the elements,
           Close over us,
           Ever eternally.

Blessing of Boats and Fishing Gear:
Roman Catholic Short Rite

Boats, fishing fleets and fishing gear receive a blessing in this short version of the Roman Catholic rite. This service is reproduced by kind permission of the International Commission on English in the Liturgy, and can also be found in the *Book of Blessings*, which also has a longer version of the blessing.[50]

Shorter Rite for the Blessing of Boats

All make the sign of the cross as the minister says:

Minister: Blessed be the name of the Lord.

Reading

Reader: Brothers and sisters, listen to the words of the holy Gospel according to Matthew (Matt. 8.23–27, NRSV): Jesus calms the storm.
And when he got into the boat, his disciples followed him. A windstorm arose on the sea, so great that the boat was being swamped by the waves; but he was asleep. And they went and woke him up, saying, 'Lord, save us! We are perishing!' And he said to them, 'Why are you afraid, you of little faith?' Then he got up and rebuked the winds and the sea; and there was a dead calm. They were amazed, saying, 'What sort of man is this, that even the winds and the sea obey him?'

Blessing

God of boundless love, at the beginning of creation your Spirit hovered over the deep. You called forth every creature, and the seas teemed with life. Through your Son, Jesus Christ, you have given us the rich harvest of salvation. Bless this boat, its equipment and all who will use it. Protect them from the dangers of wind and rain and all the perils of the deep. May Christ, who calmed the storm and filled the nets of his disciples, bring us all to the harbour of light and peace. Grant this through Christ our Lord.
Amen.

5

TREE BLESSINGS AND GATHERINGS

The spiritual power of trees and their fruit could hardly have a more prominent place at the start of the human story in the Bible: the Tree of Knowledge and its fateful crop tempting Adam and Eve. It is a theme that has been greatly amplified by subsequent Christian tradition, writers from the early church onwards identifying the wooden cross on which Christ was crucified as the Tree of Life also mentioned in Genesis. Prayers and rituals around trees are recorded from the earliest church onwards, as the following chapter illustrates.

The power of biblical tree imagery was not lost on the first Christian missionaries in the largely pagan world of northern Europe. What better way to make meaningful connections to the tree-worshipping tribal cults than to acknowledge their focus of spiritual energy was entirely well-placed, but needed further Christian interpretation to reveal its full significance. In early medieval Britain and Ireland, trees were considered a ritual place of meeting, the non-human space under the natural canopy where divine laws and concerns would predominate, where people could gather safely as equals.

One of the most important early synods in English history took place at the foot of one such landmark specimen, Augustine's Oak, named after the Roman missionary St Augustine who founded Canterbury as the capital of English Christianity. Tree veneration is less acute today, needless to say, but the ancient limbs and leafy boughs are no less loved by the general public, and no less contested too when they face threats or destruction. As a place of gathering by the wider community, therefore, to celebrate many of the outdoor liturgies in this book, they are well placed to serve as an outdoor shelter, a place of assembly unbounded by any one tradition where all may gather, where birds make their nests, as Jesus himself notes (Mark 4.30–32).

In many ways these liturgies help give focus to the significance of trees for both practical and spiritual reasons. By way of illustration of the universal nature of our need for trees, this chapter has at its heart a particularly powerful tree planting Eucharist from Africa, which has much to teach us about the theological as well as the environmental significance of trees. Tying the notion of confession to our sins against the natural world offers considerable food for thought.

The giving of a seed or sapling in a church service to mark a baptism or wedding is a modern idea that is starting to gain traction, a practice that has much to commend it. But why not follow such a gesture out of the church door and into the landscape with one of the rituals in this chapter, to ensure a planting that reminds the community of the significance of such specimens?

Liturgies in other chapters of this book pay further respect to trees. Rogation processions, for example, can pause and give a reading by an oak or other landmark tree. And in one of the blessings of apples an early liturgy makes a direct connection between the story of Adam and Eve and our own harvesting of fruit. Tree liturgies and rituals are just as accessible in an urban setting as they are in the most rural of parishes. All this is a reminder that trees have the widest possible place in the fabric of creation, larger and longer-lived than any human story could hope to contain.

A Tree-planting Liturgy

This tree-planting liturgy is a particularly poignant form of landscape ritual, combining as it does an act of remembrance with the seeding of a new tree. It has been kindly provided by Nick Utphall, pastor of the Advent Lutheran Church/Madison Christian Community in Madison, Wisconsin. Nick is also director of the Let All Creation Praise website and resource centre, which offers a range of excellent outdoor and creation-orientated material.[51]

As suggested in the introduction, the giving of a sapling or even seeds during a formal church service to mark an important event is one way to help connect the cycles of life to the rhythms of the natural world. This service could therefore be something of a counterpart to that gift made within the church building, a connected ritual that sees the new tree placed safely in the ground.

A tree planting can be held to mark all manner of events, most significantly in memory of the death of a loved one but also to mark a new beginning or a moment of transition. Another suggestion is simply to plant the tree for its own sake, a creative act that stands by itself. The service given here is shaped around the planting of a memorial tree, but could be easily adapted to other occasions.

Tree Planting

Opening song

Most hymn books will have a range of creation-facing worship songs; one popular composition suitable for an outdoor service is 'You shall go out with joy', which is based on Isaiah 55

Prayer

God of heaven and earth, the work of your hands is made known in your bountiful creation and in the lives of those who faithfully live their lives in your grace. Today we especially remember the life and work of our brother/sister [*name*], trusting your promise of everlasting life and love. Be present with us this day as we mark *their* life and remember *them* and *their* life in you through the planting of this tree. May this tree speak the power of your life in our midst, deeply rooted and ever growing in all creation, through Jesus Christ. **Amen.**

Bible reading: Isaiah 55

The following reading is suggested because of its relevance to the hymn 'You shall go out with joy', and alternative readings are Psalm 1 and John 15.1–5

Minister: Ho, everyone who thirsts,
come to the waters;
and you that have no money,
come, buy and eat!
Come, buy wine and milk
without money and without price.

Why do you spend your money for that which is not bread, and your labour for that which does not satisfy? Listen carefully to me, and eat what is good, and delight yourselves in rich food.

Incline your ear, and come to me;
listen, so that you may live.
I will make with you an everlasting covenant,
my steadfast, sure love for David.

See, I made him a witness to the peoples,
a leader and commander for the peoples.

See, you shall call nations that you do not know,
and nations that do not know you shall run to you,
because of the LORD your God, the Holy One of Israel,
for he has glorified you.

Seek the LORD while he may be found,
call upon him while he is near;

let the wicked forsake their way,
and the unrighteous their thoughts;
let them return to the LORD, that he may have mercy
on them,
and to our God, for he will abundantly pardon.

For my thoughts are not your thoughts,
nor are your ways my ways, says the LORD.

For as the heavens are higher than the earth,
so are my ways higher than your ways
and my thoughts than your thoughts.

For as the rain and the snow come down from heaven,
and do not return there until they have watered the earth,
making it bring forth and sprout,
giving seed to the sower and bread to the eater,

so shall my word be that goes out from my mouth;
it shall not return to me empty,
but it shall accomplish that which I purpose,
and succeed in the thing for which I sent it.

For you shall go out in joy,
and be led back in peace;
the mountains and the hills before you
shall burst into song,
and all the trees of the field shall clap their hands.

Instead of the thorn shall come up the cypress;
instead of the brier shall come up the myrtle;
and it shall be to the LORD for a memorial,
for an everlasting sign that shall not be cut off.

Address

On any occasion a short address is given here to talk about what is being commemorated. For a deceased person this would of course be a short eulogy, reflecting the many ways they have a lingering influence on those they have loved in this life.

Blessing of the tree

Creator of life and sustainer of seed and soil, of tree and flower, you have created this world and all that lives in it. It is to you that we come in this prayer of dedication and blessing, for you are the giver of life and the sustainer of all that lives. We come to you to dedicate this tree in memory of [*name*], who you continue to hold in your generous grace. We give you thanks for their life and come to you in our tears and sorrow. May this tree remind us of this one whom we love and who is held forever in your never-ending love. May this tree dig deep roots and grow wide branches to bear witness to your abundant love and grace made known in our brother/sister [*name*]. We ask for your blessing upon this tree and upon us who mourn, that life might dwell and bear witness to the resurrection of our Lord Jesus Christ, through whom we pray.
Amen.

Benediction and commission

May the Lord bless you and all creation with you, may the Lord care for you and keep you, may the Lord stand over you as you grow.
Go in peace. Serve the Lord, remember the poor, care for creation.

Closing song

The suggested song for closing this service is 'We shall not be moved', *which has the suitably arboreal refrain* 'Just like a tree, standing by the water'

A Tree-planting Eucharist

There can be few outdoor services that better embody the link between Christian ritual and the environment than this powerful tree-planting Eucharist, devised and celebrated by the Shona people of Zimbabwe and southern Africa.

Studied extensively by Professor Marthinus L. Daneel, who has compiled the material reproduced below, it is remarkable how far this service is integrated into an entire theology of environmental care.[52] Eucharistic services generally start with a confession of sins, which in this context has been widened to include ecological sins: 'felling trees without planting any in return; overgrazing; riverbank cultivation and neglect of contour ridges, which cause soil erosion – in other words, taking the good earth for granted and exploiting it without nurturing or reverencing it'. As Professor Daneel's study reports, there has even been talk of debarring people from receiving communion if they fail to confess these environmental sins and change their ways.

This tree-planting Eucharist is performed once a year, during the rainy season, and is explicitly an ecumenical celebration of the liturgy. The following service has been adapted with minimal changes from one conducted by Bishop Marinda in 1992, transcribed and published by Professor Daneel and reproduced here with kind permission. It takes place outdoors in a field to be planted, an area of land defined as 'God's acre' for the purposes of the liturgy. The bishop serves in the African Independent Church (AIC), an active member of the Association of African Earthkeeping Churches.

Although this precise form of Eucharistic service might not be permissible in certain church traditions, as an ordained minister will be able to advise, it is included because it makes an essential connection between the Eucharist and the wider environment, incarnational theology at its greatest reach. Liturgical material is more adaptable than is commonly recognized, this piece itself testament to a service shaped closely to local concerns and hence capable of inspiring further liturgical innovation. In this service trees are held up as part of God's creation, elevated to the point that they have communication with the prayers and worship of the faithful. It would therefore be entirely possible just to use the tree-planting ritual at the end of this liturgy if a Eucharist service is to be avoided.

Tree-planting Eucharist

Preparation

This is an outdoor service, an altar table set up on the land where the trees are to be planted. In the preparatory material for the original liturgy, this is referred to as 'God's acre'. A number of seedlings are placed on the altar at the start of the service. Seedlings or saplings are also provided for members of the congregation to pick up immediately before they go to receive communion.

Introduction

Minster: These trees will provide you with shade to protect you from the heat of the sun.
They will give you fruit, for you to lead healthy lives.

These trees will clothe the barren earth, protecting it against soil erosion, preventing it from turning into a desert, keeping the moisture in the soil. Consider the stagnant water where trees have been felled. Without trees the water sources mourn; without trees the gullies formed around the tree roots which hold the soil ... are gone!

These friends of ours give us shade.

They draw the rain clouds, breathe the moisture of rain. I, the tree ... I am your friend. I know you want wood for fire to cook your food, to warm yourself against cold.

Use my branches ... What I do not need you can have.

I, the human being, your closest friend, have committed a serious offence, I have destroyed you, our friends.

So the seedlings brought here today are the bodies of reparation.

We plant these seedlings today as an admission of guilt, strengthening our bonds with you, our tree friends of the heart.

Let us make an oath today that we will care for God's creation so that he will grant us rain.

An oath, not in jest, but with all our heart admitting our guilt, appeasing the aggrieved spirit, offering our trees in earnest to clothe the barren land.

Indeed, there were forests, abundance of rain.

But in our ignorance and greed we left the land naked.

Like a person in shame our country is shy of its nakedness.

Our planting of trees today is a sign of harmony between us and creation.

We are reconciled with creation through the body and blood of Jesus which brings peace, he who came to save all creation (Col. 1.19–20).

Reading

Reader: A reading from the book of Genesis 2.15–17.
The LORD God took the man and put him in the garden of Eden to till it and keep it. And the LORD God commanded the man, 'You may freely eat of every tree of the garden; but of the tree of the knowledge of good and evil you shall not eat, for in the day that you eat of it you shall die.'

Minister: Peace to you!
It says that God placed man in the garden to work it and take care of it. But man did not obey God's commandment. Instead, he violated God's law. The devil used man to rebel against God and creation. Man became an enemy by cutting down all the trees. As a result the weather patterns of the entire world changed. Man became the destroyer of the rain forests, the killer of the world's ecosystems.

So today we confess to you, our God, our sins of wantonly chopping down trees. We confess our abuse of creation; sins which have caused us to lose good pasture for our cattle and fertile topsoil for our crops. Bad farming methods brought this about. Today the cattle are feeding on soil, O Lord, because there is no grass. God, you are punishing us with severe drought because we have denuded the land. Look, the rivers are dried up and all the fish have gone, because we cut away all the vegetation on the riverbanks, causing the riverbeds to fill up with sand. People are dying every day because they breathe polluted air. There are no trees to clear the air polluted by smoke from our factories. The trees are our friends who eat the poisoned air and give us fresh air to breathe in return. The clean air gives us life!

Reading

Reader: A reading from Paul's letter to the Colossians 1.15–20. He is the image of the invisible God, the firstborn of all creation; for in him all things in heaven and on earth were created, things visible and invisible, whether thrones or dominions or rulers or powers – all things have been created through him and for him. He himself is before all things, and in him all things hold together. He is the head of the body, the church; he is the beginning, the firstborn from the dead, so that he might come to have first place in everything. For in him all the fullness of God was pleased to dwell, and through him God was pleased to reconcile to himself all things, whether on earth or in heaven, by making peace through the blood of his cross.

Minister: There are millions of creatures which we cannot even see with our naked eyes. We only observe them with the aid of microscopes. All these beings were created by God. Because we need order everyone must submit to the governing authority. These people were given authority by God, for there is no authority other than that established by God. Those who disobey such authority are rebelling against God and will bring judgement on themselves. We rebel against God by not keeping the environment as God instructed us. The devil is at war with God and the devil is using people to destroy all of creation. This drought which has brought untold suffering to our people, to the animals, the fish in the water and the birds in the air, is God's judgement on the environmental sins we have committed.

Confession

Let us all confess our sins, so that our sins through the love of God in Christ may be forgiven.

In Jesus Christ all things hold together, as it says in Colossians 1.17. He is the head of the body, the church. He is the beginning of all creation and he reigns supreme. God reconciled all things in heaven and on earth with himself through Christ. Christ is Lord over all creation. He works salvation for all humans because humans are the crown of creation. Humans in turn have the duty to extend salvation to all of creation as Christ's co-workers.

If we look at the history of sin offerings in the Old Testament, we are told that each person had to bring an animal or bird to be offered at the Tent of Meeting before the Lord. The priest had to burn these sacrificial animals on a wood fire on the altar of burnt offerings. This was in fact a cruel practice, because many animals and birds had to die for the iniquities of humans. Trees were felled in great numbers to provide firewood for the burnt offerings. Christ came as the last offering, to forgive the sins of the entire world. Through his death on the cross he saved the animals, the birds and the trees. So he saves his entire creation! The plan of God's salvation of humanity through Jesus Christ included the salvation of all creation.

The liturgy

The holy communion of which we partake today introduces us to the new Eucharist of tree planting. On the night Jesus was betrayed he took bread, broke it, and said: 'This is my body, which is for you. Eat it in remembrance of me.'

Then he took the cup of wine, saying: 'This is the new covenant in my blood; whenever you drink it, remember me.' For whenever you eat this bread and drink this cup, you proclaim the Lord's death until he comes.

Jesus one day went down to Capernaum with his mother, brothers and disciples. It was about time for the Jewish Passover. In the temple he found people selling cattle, sheep and doves. These were to be used as sin offerings. When Jesus heard the lowing and bleating he knew the poor creatures were crying to be saved from the cruel merchants – they who had turned God's holy dwelling into a marketplace of debauchery.

So Jesus made a whip out of cords and lashed the corrupt merchants until they fled. He saved the animals and birds from the cruel fate that awaited them. Christ came to save all creation. Through his blood, the animals, the birds, the trees were saved.

Since then, in the new covenant, people no longer bring live sin offerings to have their sins forgiven. Our Eucharist of tree planting symbolizes Christ's salvation of all creation, for in him all things hold together.

Let us celebrate this Eucharist with humble hearts, confessing our wanton tree felling without replacing any in return.

There was war in heaven, says the Bible. He was hurled down, that ancient serpent called Satan, he who leads the whole world astray. So the devil is deceiving the whole world causing humans to fight creation. Possessed by the demon humans are destroying nature's beauty.

All living things suffer – the trees, the animals, water. It shall continue until humans extinguish all life on earth.

If we continue to kill the trees we hurt ourselves by hastening the end of the world.

If the world is ultimately destroyed it will be the doing of humans.

Communicants come up to the altar to receive the Eucharist, carrying a sapling, seedling or seed that they will plant

The tree planting ceremony

Before the seedlings are planted, the minister walks around the plot sprinkling holy water on the ground and on the seedlings

> This is the water of purification and fertility.
> We sprinkle it on this new acre of trees.
> It is a prayer to God, a symbol of rain so that the trees will grow, so that the land will heal as the darkness we have caused withdraws.

'Holy soil' which has been prayed over is then scattered over the ground

> You soil, I bless you in the name of Christ for you to make the trees grow and to protect them. Provide the trees with sufficient food for proper growth.
> Love the trees and keep their roots for they are our friends.

Members of the congregation then join in a prayer for their own seedlings to be planted

> You, tree, my brother, my sister, today I plant you in this soil.
> I shall give water for your growth.
> Have good roots to keep the soil from eroding.
> Have many leaves and branches
> so that we can breathe fresh air,
> sit in your shade,
> and find firewood.
> Amen.

A Toast to a Tree

One of the most obscure of all landscape blessings must be the practice of raising a toast to a fruit-bearing tree. This ritual, for it just about merits the description, was an offshoot of the popular custom of 'wassailing' or 'howling', which involved going round the local area and toasting good health to the community on the Twelfth Night (5 January). Frequently recorded in the early modern period, this folk tradition involved visiting a fruit orchard and drinking cider three times as a toast. In Sussex and Surrey a clear Christian gloss was added to the most common form of words, farmers and workmen circling the tree three times before their triple toast, reciting the following rhyme. For full details of this tradition and many other folk landscape rituals and superstitions see the extensive compilation *Stations of the Sun* by Ronald Hutton.[53]

Toast to a Tree

Stand fast root, bear well top
Pray the God send us a howling good crop.
Every twig, apples big,
Every bough, apples now.
Here's to thee, old apple tree,
Whence thou mayst bud
And whence thou mayst blow!
And whence thou mayst bear apples enow!
Hats full! Caps full!
Bushel – bushel – sacks full,
And my pockets full too! Huzza!

A Prayer Over Trees and Vines

This prayer is from the Orthodox Christian book known as *Trebnik* or *Euchologion*, a collection of all the main liturgies used in the Eastern Orthodox churches. Much of the material dates back to the earliest centuries of the Christian church, with liturgical material written by St John Chrysostom and St Basil of Caesarea in the fourth and fifth centuries. The following prayer can be said in an orchard or vineyard, reflecting some of the many outdoor settings in which this liturgical book is used.[54]

1 A Prayer Over Vines

Minister: Let us pray to the Lord.
All: **Lord have mercy.**

Bless, O Lord, this new fruit of the vine, which through the purity of the air, and through showers of rain and temperate weather, you are well-pleased should at this time attain unto maturity. May our partaking of this new growth of the vine be for gladness, and for the offering of a gift to you for the cleansing of sins, through the sacred and holy body of your Christ, with whom you are blessed, together with your most holy, and good, and life-creating Spirit, now and ever, and to the ages of ages.
Amen.

2 A Prayer Over Fruit-bearing Trees

Minister: Let us pray to the Lord.
All: **Lord have mercy.**

Bless, O Lord, this new fruit of the tree, which through the purity of the air, and through showers of rain and temperate weather, you are well-pleased should at this time attain unto maturity. May our partaking of this new growth of the tree be for gladness, through the sacred and holy body of your Christ, with whom you are blessed, together with your most holy, and good, and life-creating Spirit, now and ever, and to the ages of ages.
Amen.

An Early Medieval Tree Blessing

This short formula for blessing an apple tree is taken from one of the oldest surviving liturgical texts, the *Gelasian Sacramentary*, the oldest copy of which dates from around AD 750.[55] It is named after the fifth-century Pope Gelasius I and even though there is no evidence that he was personally connected to its creation it is thought to represent mainstream Roman liturgical practice in early medieval Europe. As such, this prayer is an important artefact of nature-facing liturgy, and could easily be used to bless any type of fruit or nut tree.

A Tree Blessing

God who wished for this [apple] tree to grow, by your command and providence, we pray you now also to bless and worthily sanctify it that whoever eats from it may be strong and unimpaired.
Through Jesus Christ our Lord, who with the Father and Holy Spirit is worshipped and glorified, one God now and forever.
Amen.

6

FIELDS, HILLS, WEATHER
AND AGRICULTURE

From the flattest of water meadows to the highest of peaks, spiritual significance clings to the landscape as it has done since time immemorial. While most of the rituals celebrating the natural world focus on agriculture, for obvious reasons of human need, there is much more to be found besides in this collection of liturgies celebrating wide open rural land, creation blessed for its own sake.

Field blessings are to be found in the very earliest of Christian writings in Britain. Around the year AD 700 the *Life of St Columba* records how the community of Iona Monastery conducted a powerful and seemingly effective ritual procession around their island in order to ward off a drought. As it is the earliest complete description of a landscape liturgy in a British context, it merits repetition here in full. Faced with parched fields and dying crops, the monks hit upon this ritual plan involving the personal possessions of the monastery's founder St Columba:

> Some of our elders should walk around the fields that had lately been ploughed and sown, carrying with them St Columba's white tunic and books which the saint had himself copied. They should hold aloft the tunic, which was the one he wore at the hour of his departure from the flesh, and shake it three times. They should open his books and read aloud from them at the Hill of Angels, where from

time to time the citizens of heaven used to be seen coming down to converse with the saint.[56]

In many ways the landscape rituals in this chapter and this book help to break down the strict division between ritual conducted within the four walls of the church building and the spiritual significance of the world outside. To that end, it is suggested that any church liturgy conducted in advance of a procession or movement into the landscape in order to celebrate one of the rituals in this chapter, parishioners could bring their own garden seeds for a blessing, and crosses can also be blessed for parishioners to take home and plant in the fields or their own gardens.

Making these crosses, out of twigs or dried grass, would be a good project for the children of the church school or individual families. Instructions for creating a Brigid's Cross out of reeds can readily be found online, an ancient Celtic piece of craft that uses only natural materials. As one of the most exotic rituals in this chapter, the Æcerbot, testifies, the practice of planting or burying small crosses in four corners of a patch of land has a long pedigree as a landscape ritual. This would be a gentle way of evoking the power of our most ancient landscape liturgies.

The full Æcebot ritual might be a stretch for modern Christians today but it certainly had the full backing of the church in earlier times. Professor Karen Jolly, an expert in the matter of early landscape lore, has argued convincingly that it is meaningless to attempt to distinguish pagan from Christian elements in such early recorded rituals.[57] One could easily claim that the Æcerbot shows hallmarks of pagan survivals from folk magic and superstitions, but the Christian elements are highly pronounced and overt: Christian theology and even cosmology are an inseparable part of the ritual language and action. Whether or not you could find a priest willing to offer a church and altar to put it into practice again today is however a moot point. It is perhaps the least likely of all the rituals in this book to see a revival, but its age and overwhelming sense of spiritual power in the landscape alone should give pause for thought, if not a full reconstruction.

When it comes to hills and mountaintops, whatever ritual practice there was has fallen into even greater disuse than agricultural and weather rituals. Yet just enough evidence from place names, archaeology and the written record survives to allow one suggested service to be proposed here. Some of south-west Britain's most iconic hilltops are crowned with an ancient chapel or church building, and a quick look through a list of their names reveals a common theme: dedications to the Archangel St Michael. From the ruined tower of St Michael's Church on Glastonbury Tor in Somerset to the chapel at the heart of the castle on St Michael's Mount in Cornwall along with many other less striking summits, it is clear that some sort of ancient landscape spirituality clings to the UK's lofty peaks.

One such chapel, again dedicated to St Michael, leaves its trace at the top of the striking holy mountain of Skirrid, near Abergavenny in Monmouthshire, barely more than a handful of dressed stones. It was here in the 1680s that a local MP complained that 'Papists' were gathering to conduct services and say prayers, leading to a witch hunt that ended in the death of a Roman Catholic priest, the martyred St David Lewis. It was the tradition to climb the hill after dark on the eve of Michaelmas, which is celebrated on 29 September, to hold a clandestine Mass in the ancient chapel here, now all but obliterated from the landscape.

It has been claimed that the Archangel's cult on top of hills reflects that fact that pre-Christian temples were once sited there. St Michael appears in the book of Revelation casting down Satan from the 'high place' that is heaven, so it is assumed that his name is evoked to reflect the overthrow of 'demonic' pagan sites, particularly ones in a lofty position. There is not really enough evidence to support such a claim, colourful though the story is.

Those wishing to honour St Michael, or indeed the devotees who risked their lives to visit these hilltop chapels, may be interested in using the old form of Catholic liturgy for Michaelmas included here, which would have shaped such clandestine worship. A modern Michaelmas Day liturgy would serve much the same function.

A Service for the Apparition of
St Michael the Archangel

This liturgy comes from a nineteenth-century Mass book, which contains two services in honour of St Michael the Archangel. Both of them use pretty much the same words, give or take the odd seasonal 'alleluia', as noted in the text below, and are effectively a single liturgy which can be put to general use.

The first feast day is on 8 May and is a celebration of the apparition of St Michael. This actually occurred on the opposite side of the English Channel from St Michael's Mount in Cornwall, at its counterpart monastic island of Mont St Michel in France. In the year AD 708 a local bishop saw a vision of the Archangel instructing him to build a monastery on the tidal island. Perhaps it was this famous apparition, along with the striking image of a monastic church perched atop a wave-washed crag, that inspired so many other hilltop chapels to be given the same dedication over in southern England and Wales.

The second feast day celebrated with a Mass is of course the more famous festival of Michaelmas, which takes place on 29 September. This marks the date on which a basilica in Rome was dedicated to the Archangel in the fifth century. The liturgy reproduced here is found in an Irish Roman Catholic Missal.[58] Although it has the shape of a Mass that would end with Communion, the readings and prayers are of general use and could be used alone for a short hilltop service without the concluding communion and post-communion prayers.

A Hilltop Service for St Michael

Psalm 103

> Bless the LORD, O you his angels,
>> you mighty ones who do his bidding,
>> obedient to his spoken word.
> Bless the LORD, all his hosts,
>> his ministers that do his will.
> Bless the LORD, all his works,
>> in all places of his dominion.
> Bless the LORD, O my soul.

All: **Glory to the Father, and to the Son, and to the Holy Spirit: as it was in the beginning, is now, and will be for ever. Amen.**

Collect

God, who disposes in a wonderful order the services of angels and of men; grant in your mercy, that those who ever stand before your face to minister to you in heaven may protect us during our life on earth. **Through our Lord Jesus Christ, your Son, who lives and reigns with you and the Holy Spirit, one God, forever and ever.**

Reader: A reading from the Revelation of St John 1.1–5.
The revelation of Jesus Christ, which God gave him to show his servants what must soon take place; he made it known by sending his angel to his servant John, who testified to the word of God and to the testimony of Jesus Christ, even to all that he saw. Blessed is the one who reads aloud the words of the prophecy, and blessed are those who hear and who keep what is written in it; for the time is near. John to the seven churches that are in Asia: 'Grace to you and peace from him who is and who was and who is to come, and from the seven spirits who are before his throne, and from Jesus Christ, the faithful witness, the firstborn of the dead, and the ruler of the kings of the earth. To him who loves us and freed us from our sins by his blood.'

(During Eastertide the following two verses and responses are used)

Alleluia, Alleluia.
Holy Archangel Michael, defend us in the battle that we
may not perish in the dreadful judgement.
Alleluia.
The sea was shaken, and the earth trembled when the
Archangel Michael came down from heaven.
Alleluia.

*(Out of Eastertide, the following gradual is used instead of the two
verses and responses above)*

Bless the Lord, all you his angels. You who are mighty in
strength, who do his will.
Bless the Lord, O my soul, and all that is within me, bless
his holy name.
Alleluia, Alleluia. *(Omitted at Michaelmas)*
Holy Archangel Michael, defend us in the battle, that we
may not perish in the dreadful judgement.
Alleluia. *(Omitted at Michaelmas)*

Gospel reading

Reader: A reading from the Gospel according to Matthew 18.1–10.
At that time the disciples came to Jesus and asked, 'Who is
the greatest in the kingdom of heaven?' He called a child,
whom he put among them, and said, 'Truly I tell you, unless
you change and become like children, you will never enter
the kingdom of heaven. Whoever becomes humble like this
child is the greatest in the kingdom of heaven. Whoever
welcomes one such child in my name welcomes me.

'If any of you put a stumbling block before one of these
little ones who believe in me, it would be better for you if
a great millstone were fastened around your neck and you
were drowned in the depth of the sea. Woe to the world
because of stumbling blocks! Occasions for stumbling
are bound to come, but woe to the one by whom the
stumbling block comes!

'If your hand or your foot causes you to stumble, cut it off
and throw it away; it is better for you to enter life maimed
or lame than to have two hands or two feet and to be
thrown into the eternal fire. And if your eye causes you to
stumble, tear it out and throw it away; it is better for you

to enter life with one eye than to have two eyes and to be thrown into the hell of fire.

'Take care that you do not despise one of these little ones; for, I tell you, in heaven their angels continually see the face of my Father in heaven.'

Creed

We believe in one God,
the Father, the Almighty,
maker of heaven and earth,
of all that is, seen and unseen.
We believe in one Lord, Jesus Christ,
the only Son of God,
eternally begotten of the Father,
God from God, Light from Light,
true God from true God,
begotten, not made,
of one Being with the Father.
Through him all things were made.
For us and for our salvation
he came down from heaven:
by the power of the Holy Spirit
he became incarnate from the Virgin Mary,
and was made man.
For our sake he was crucified under Pontius Pilate;
he suffered death and was buried.
On the third day he rose again
in accordance with the Scriptures;
he ascended into heaven
and is seated at the right hand of the Father.
He will come again in glory to judge the living and the dead,
and his kingdom will have no end.
We believe in the Holy Spirit, the Lord, the giver of life,
who proceeds from the Father and the Son.
With the Father and the Son he is worshipped and glorified.
He has spoken through the Prophets.
We believe in one holy catholic and apostolic Church.
We acknowledge one baptism for the forgiveness of sins.
We look for the resurrection of the dead,
and the life of the world to come.
Amen.

Offertory

Reader: A reading from the Revelation of St John 8.3–4.
Another angel with a golden censer came and stood at
the altar; he was given a great quantity of incense to offer
with the prayers of all the saints on the golden altar that is
before the throne. And the smoke of the incense, with the
prayers of the saints, rose before God from the hand of the
angel.
Alleluia. *(Omitted at Michaelmas)*

Secret

We offer you a sacrifice of praise, O Lord, and humbly beseech that,
through the prayers of your holy angels, who plead for us, you would
graciously receive it, and grant that it may avail our salvation.
**Through our Lord Jesus Christ, your Son, who lives and reigns with
you and the Holy Spirit, one God, forever and ever.**

For a Eucharistic service only

*The following can be omitted unless a priest or minister is present to
conduct a full Communion*

Communion prayer

All you angels of the Lord, bless the Lord, sing a hymn, and exalt
him above all for ever.
Alleluia.

Post-Communion

Relying, O Lord, on the intercession of your blessed Archangel
Michael, we humbly beseech you that the sacrament which has
passed our lips may quicken our souls.
**Through our Lord Jesus Christ, your Son, who lives and reigns with
you and the Holy Spirit, one God, forever and ever.**

Field Blessings from Anglo-Saxon England

75 The fully developed medieval plough, | with ox-team, ploughshare and mouldboard (an illumination from the Luttrell Psalter)

The following is an enigmatic collection of blessings which were written around the year AD 970 as an addition to a manuscript of rituals kept at Durham Cathedral. The prayers imply that a number of ritual actions were used, including the sprinkling of holy water over crops, although they are not directly described in any rubric. There are several unusual features such as the invocation of the 'Archangel Panchiel' and references to the seldom-quoted book of Tobit, one of the marginal books in the Hebrew Bible, whose charm against a demon using fish entrails is described in Tobit 6.17–18. These prayers have been diligently and lucidly analysed and translated by Professor Karen Jolly, and are reproduced here by her kind permission.[59]

The name Archangel Panchiel only appears in one other manuscript from this period, from Germany, a tantalizing glimpse of belief in a whole range of angelic beings with specific powers, in this case crop protection. The final prayer is particularly unusual in that it blesses breadcrumbs to be sprinkled on crops as a means of warding off birds, a counterintuitive suggestion if ever there was one. It is possible that the bread could have been burnt at the field in order to fumigate the crops, a rich and redolent collapse of bread and incense into one liturgical element. Bread would burn better if dried thoroughly beforehand.

The Field Blessings

Minister: Christ be blessed.

The following prayer is said over the 'creature', which means the water to be sprinkled over the crops for their protection:

To God omnipotent, to you Lord God we pray, who have named your son Jesus Christ with twelve names. Therefore I adjure you creature of water through the Archangel Panchiel that these may be burned up and put to flight: demons and flying things, worms and rodents, and all venomous animals from our fields, in the name of God the Father and Son and Holy Spirit, [you] who reign forever and ever.

Another prayer over the water for protection from birds

Creator and protector of humankind, giver of spiritual grace, bestower of eternal salvation, send forth your Holy Spirit over this creature of water so that armed with the virtue of heavenly defence it may benefit the health of soul and body, through [our] Lord [Jesus Christ].

Another prayer for the crops

Holy Lord, Father omnipotent, eternal God, send forth your Holy Spirit with the Archangel Panchiel that he may defend our crops from worms, from winged things, from demons, from lightning bolts, from all temptations of the devil, by the invocation of your holy name, Jesus Christ, [you] who reign with the Father and who live with the Holy Spirit, forever and ever.

Another prayer over seeds

We pray you Lord holy Father omnipotent, eternal God: reproduce fertile seed, as in your name Panchiel wishes, who is over all fruits of the earth and over seeds, along with forty-four thousand angels, so that this creature may take root or, cast upon the earth, may remain unharmed. May your name be magnified in all the earth, or in all places so that the people will know that there is no other God beside you. Through God omnipotent and through the Lord of lords and through his son Jesus Christ who called the twelve apostles by [their] names. Therefore I adjure you creature of water that the Lord command neither evil nor disease; nor temptation be allowed to operate in this field. Rather, just as the demon Asmodeus who was driven out by the fish gall through the Archangel Raphael, so may the birds be driven out from our crops. And may this creature be beneficial for putting to flight and expelling the demon, in the name of God the Father and Son and Holy Spirit.

Another prayer over bread and water to be sprinkled

Through the Lord Father omnipotent, you who have named your son with twelve names, I adjure you creature of bread that you be a fire burning against snares of the devil and winged things, just as the demon Asmodeus fled, who was driven out by the fish gall through the Archangel Raphael, so may winged things be driven out from our crops. In the name of God, Father and Son and Holy Spirit. Lord, deign to bless our crop through this creature of water and through the blessing which we bless so that the flying things of the sky and birds of the earth be overthrown from them through the invocation of your name, Father and Son and Holy Spirit.

The Prayer of St Tryphon for the Protection of Gardens, Fields and Crops

Gardeners and other growers have long been thankful for the intercessions of St Tryphon, to whom this prayer is tradition-ally addressed by the Orthodox Church, seeking protection for crops from pests. St Tryphon was born in Campsada, a town in the central region of modern-day Turkey, and was martyred by beheading during the persecutions under Emperor Decius around the year AD 250. Numer-ous colourful legends remain of his life, which emphasize his miraculous abilities to heal animals.

He is to this day considered patron saint of gardeners and wine growers in the Orthodox Church, and also patron saint of birds in Russia, and is widely venerated in other Christian traditions. His feast day is 1 February. The prayer is preserved in the writings of St Nikodemos the Hagiorite, who compiled anthologies of many great early Christian texts on Mount Athos in the early nineteenth century. It is reproduced here with kind permission from the resources of the Pan-Orthodox Concern for Animals, a charity based in the UK; more details about the charity can be found on page 33.

Prayer of St Tryphon

Most-glorious martyr of Christ and soldier of the heavenly King, Tryphon most-blessed, namesake of the eternal sustenance, who bravely confessed Christ upon the earth, and for this ever receives unfading blessedness in the heavens, and with boldness stands before the throne of the three-sun Godhead. Your greatness as martyr we take refuge in after God, all of us sinners and your unworthy servants, and we entreat your sympathetic and Christ-like philanthropy, that, having compassion upon us who are in danger and trouble, you may drive far from our fields and gardens and vineyards, all reptiles, and locusts, and caterpillars, and various species of insects and beasts, the diseases of fruit and leaves and roots of trees, and all vegetables and seeds and legumes of ours. For to you was granted this special and unique grace, O great champion, by our Saviour Jesus Christ. Not only while still living, through your God-pleasing life, but more so now after your death through martyrdom and through blood, confessed him and persevered for the faith.

Yes, we confess that through our sins we have been delivered up to these such sorrows, and we have fallen under God's anger. But you O brave champion, only desiring your boldness as a martyr is needed; we believe that you easily extinguish the injunction against us by God and transform our faint-heartedness into good-heartedness. Therefore, because of our sins, we have no boldness to stand before your champion-like glory, and immediately have you make intercession, therefore we place your blood, which you O all-famed one shed for Christ as our intercessor instead, and the struggles which you endured as a martyr in your most-suffering body.

Therefore look down, O most-compassionate martyr, upon these, for you confessed Christ and received the unfading crown of martyrdom, and hearken to the prayer from your humble supplicants, and deliver from the present dangers of reptiles and locusts and beasts and various vermin, of those that ruin the fruits of our fields and vineyards and gardens. For we are in danger by them of starvation and death and being left utterly desolate, if it were not for your compassions speedily granted to all of us, that through your ready protection, driving away the coming danger, we may ceaselessly and necessarily magnify your name, our saviour and benefactor and helper whom we ascribe after God, and through you we glorify the common master, our Lord Jesus Christ, who is glorified on earth and in heaven. To whom belongs all glory, honour and worship, with the Father and the Holy Spirit, unto the ages.
All: Amen.

Blessing of Seeds at Planting Time: Short Order Roman Catholic Rite

Prayers and blessings at the start of the growing season are traditional in many agricultural communities. Although less commonly practised than the Harvest Festival celebrations at the end of the season, blessing ceremonies for seeds are an important way to inaugurate the time of planting and growth. The service is reproduced by kind permission of the International Commission on English in the Liturgy, and can also be found in the *Book of Blessings*, which also has a longer version of the blessing.[60]

The Blessing of Seeds

All make the sign of the cross as the minister says:

Minister: Our help is in the name of the Lord.
All: Who made heaven and earth.

Reading

Reader: Brothers and sisters, listen to the words of the first letter of Paul to the Corinthians (1 Cor. 15.35–39):
But someone will ask, 'How are the dead raised? With what kind of body do they come?' Fool! What you sow does not come to life unless it dies. And as for what you sow, you do not sow the body that is to be, but a bare seed, perhaps of wheat or of some other grain. But God gives it a body as he has chosen, and to each kind of seed its own body. Not all flesh is alike, but there is one flesh for human beings, another for animals, another for birds, and another for fish.

The prayer of blessing

Lord of the harvest, you placed the gifts of creation in our hands and called us to till the earth and make it fruitful. We ask your blessing as we prepare to place these seeds (seedlings) in the earth. May the care we show these seeds (seedlings) remind us of your tender love for your people. We ask this through Christ our Lord.
Amen.

The Æcerbot Field Blessing Ritual

No British book on landscape liturgies could be complete without including the mysterious Æcerbot ritual from Anglo-Saxon England, which seeks to remove a curse from an area of farmland. It survives in written form in an eleventh-century manuscript. The suggestive mix of Christian ritual, indecipherable chants, and the application of an exotic mix of materials to the soil defies easy attempts to categorize this in terms of religious tradition. It certainly presents itself as a thoroughly Christian ritual, but it would take a broad-minded believer today to accommodate such a curious mix of symbolism and language. In particular, the three-fold chant of *erce, erce, erce* has so far defied the best efforts of translators and commentators, a word that is of unknown origin and meaning.

The text below has been translated by Professor Karen Jolly, an expert on the period and a kind supporter of this project.[61] Professor Jolly has envisioned the possibility of revival of the full ritual, but points out that it would need to take place across two days. It would also need the support of a broad-minded church, happy to house the part of the service which requires an altar: four sods cut from the field being blessed need to be placed in the church with the grassy surface facing the four sides of the altar table, and Masses sung over them.

The text refers to several conventional Christian prayers which are still in use today: the *Sanctus* prayer ('Holy, holy, holy…'), the *Magnificat* of Mary, the *Pater noster* (Lord's Prayer), and the *Benedicite* ('Bless the Lord all you works of the Lord…'). The litanies referred to are a form of prayer which invokes a number of saints (if performing this service, you could use the Catholic Litany of the Saints: 'St Peter, pray for us. St Andrew, pray for us. St John, pray for us…').

At least one recreation of this ritual has been carried out in the modern era, in Suffolk in 2013. Perhaps unsurprisingly, the information about that revival fails to record which altar was used, or indeed to mention any church building at all, perhaps indicating ecclesiastical reluctance to be seen to endorse this extraordinary Æcerbot.[62]

Yet there are elements to recommend this most earthy of rituals even to a modern community. It helps to break down the demarcation between parish and church, the field ritual spilling without inhibition into and back out of the church building. The application of milk and honey to the soil is surely an evocation of the Holy Land itself, layers of time and space collapsing in the weight of God's promise to provide. And finally we have bread itself as perhaps the ultimate symbol of God's presence in physical form, from field to altar to field, liturgical action and meaning stretched far beyond their usual bounds to touch and grace all of creation.

The Æcerbot Ritual

Here is the remedy, how you may better your land, if it will not grow well, or if some harmful thing has been done to it by a sorcerer or by a poisoner.

Take then at night, before it dawns, four sods from four sides of the land, and mark how they stood before.

Take then oil and honey and yeast, and milk of each livestock that is on the land, and a piece of each tree type that grows on the land, except hard beams, and a piece of each plant known by name, except glappan[63] *only, and put then holy water thereon, and drip then three times on the base of the sods, and say then these words:*

[bilingual Latin and Old English:] *Crescite*, grow, et *multiplicamini*, and multiply, et *replete*, and fill, *terre*, the earth. *In nomine patris et filii et spiritus sancti sit benedicti.* And [say] the *Pater noster* as often as the other.

And bear afterward the sods into church, and have a masspriest sing four masses over the sods, and have someone turn the green [sides] to the altar, and afterward have someone bring the sods to where they were before, before sunset.

And have made for them of quickbeam four Christ's signs [wooden crosses], and write on each end: Matthew and Mark, Luke and John. Lay that Christ's sign in the bottom of the pit, saying then: Crux Matheus, Crux Marcus, Crux Lucas, Crux Sanctus Iohannes.

Take then the sods and set them down there on [the crosses], and say then nine times these words: Crescite [grow], *and as often the* Pater noster, *and turn yourself then eastward, and bow nine times humbly, and say then these words:*

Eastward I stand, for mercies I pray,
I pray the great *domine* [lord], I pray the powerful lord,
I pray the holy guardian of heaven-kingdom,
earth I pray and sky

and the true *sancta* [holy] Mary
and heaven's might and high hall,
that I may this *galdor*[64] by the gift of the lord
open with [my] teeth through firm thought,
to call forth these plants for our worldly use,
to fill this land with firm belief,
to beautify this grassy sod, as the wiseman said
that he would have riches on earth who alms
gave with justice by the grace of the lord.

*Turn then thrice with the sun's course, stretch then out lengthwise,
and recite there the litanies, and say then:* Sanctus, sanctus, sanctus *to
the end. Sing then* Benedicite *with outstretched arms, and* Magnificat,
and Pater noster *thrice, and commend it [the land] to Christ, and
Saint Mary, and the holy cross, for praise, and for worship, and for
the benefit of the one who owns that land and all those who are
serving under him.*

*When all that is done, then have someone take unknown seed from
almsmen, and give them twice as much as the person took from them,
and have him gather all his plough tools together. Bore then in the
beam [of the plough, putting in?] incense and fennel and hallowed
soap and hallowed salt. Take then that seed, set it on the plough's
body, say then:*

Erce, Erce, Erce, earth's mother,
May the all-ruler grant you, the eternal lord,
fields growing and flourishing,
propagating and strengthening,
tall shafts, bright crops,
and broad barley crops,
and white wheat crops,
and all earth's crops.
May the eternal lord grant him,
and his holy ones, who are in heaven,
that his produce be guarded against any enemies whatsoever,
and that it be safe against any harm at all,
from poisons sown around the land.
Now I bid the ruler, who shaped this world,
that there be no speaking-woman nor artful man
that can overturn these words thus spoken.

Then have someone drive forth the plough and the first furrow cut.
Say then:

Whole may you be earth, mother of men!
May you be growing in God's embrace,
with food filled for the needs of men.
Take then each kind of flour, and have someone bake a loaf [the size
of] a hand's palm, and knead it with milk and with holy water, and
lay it under the first furrow. Say then:
Field full of food for mankind,
bright-blooming, you are blessed
in the holy name of the one who shaped heaven
and the earth on which we live;
the God, the one who made the ground, grant us the gift of growing,
that for us each grain might come to use.
Say then thrice:
Crescite in nomine patris, sit benedicti. [Grow in the name of the
father, be blessed].
[Say also] Amen and *Pater noster* three times.

Blessing of First Grain and Blessing of a Bakery

These two short blessing services have been kindly provided by the Dean of Southwark Cathedral. Both are conducted on the ancient festival of Lammas Day, which occurs on 1 August. The word 'Lammas' derives from the Anglo-Saxon term *hlaf-mas*, or 'loaf-mass', referring to the church service when the first fruits of the growing season are gathered in, and thanks given in a Mass.

Although located in the most urban of settings, Southwark Cathedral exemplifies a creation-facing ritual life in a number of ways, including these two grain and bakery blessings and an annual blessing service over the River Thames (see page 114). It has also in recent years celebrated its cathedral cat, Doorkins Magnificat, a stray who was adopted by the cathedral's staff, congregation and visitors alike, and much mourned at her death in 2020.

1 The Blessing of the Grain for the First Milling

Moses said to the people 'When anyone presents a grain-offering to the LORD, the offering shall be of choice flour.' (Lev. 2.1)

Jesus said 'The earth produces of itself, first the stalk, then the head, then the full grain in the head.' (Mark 4.28)

Let us give thanks for this grain of the new harvest to be milled to make choice flour which will be baked into the Lammas loaf.

All: Lord of the harvest,
                bless the grain now in our hand
                bless the miller in their work
                bless the baker in their task
                bless the bread that will be baked
                bless the people to be fed
                bless the world you love so much
                and all in the name of Jesus our Lord.
                Amen.

2 *Blessing of a Bakery*

God said to Moses, 'The best of the first fruits of your ground you shall bring to the house of the LORD your God.' (Ex. 34.26)

On this Lammas Day as we prepare to take a loaf, baked with the first flour of this new harvest, into the cathedral and to the table where bread is broken and wine is shared, where Christ makes himself known and feeds his people, we ask God's blessing on this bakery for the coming year.

Almighty God,
whose Son broke bread
to feed the thousands
and to feed his friends;
bless this bakery,
those who work in it
and those who enjoy the bread
from its ovens.
May we be proved as is the dough,
rise in heart and spirit
and so be fed by daily bread
that we may live to your glory
feed the hungry
and make known your goodness
now and for ever.
Amen.

A Reaping Blessing from the
Carmina Gadelica

This blessing for a bountiful harvest is included in the extensive collection of oral traditions from the Gaelic-speaking Highlands and Islands gathered by the Scottish writer Alexander Carmichael, which he called the *Carmina Gadelica*.[65] This four-stanza poetic prayer is directed towards God, and concludes with a stanza that reads more or less like a traditional litany, a form of prayer in which saints are invoked and asked for their aid; the 'Bride' mentioned is St Brigid.

There is also an action connected to this prayer, a harvest ritual that was conducted in the field. Carmichael's introduction indicates that the intercessor would remove their hat, turn to face the sun, and wind a handful of the 'corn', more likely wheat or barley, three times around their head in a 'sunwise' (clockwise) direction. Other suggested actions include throwing sickles in the air, which is probably best left safely in the nineteenth century; the orientation towards the sun is sufficient to engage the body in meaningful relationship to the natural world.

Reaping Blessing

God, bless thou thyself my reaping,
Each ridge, and plain, and field.
Each sickle curved, shapely, hard,
Each ear and handful in the sheaf.
   Each ear and handful in the sheaf.

Bless each maiden and youth,
Each woman and tender youngling,
Safeguard them beneath thy shield of strength,
And guard them in the house of the saints,
   Guard them in the house of the saints.

Encompass each goat, sheep and lamb,
Each cow and horse, and store,
Surround thou the flocks and herds,
And tend them to a kindly fold,
   Tend them to a kindly fold.

For the sake of Michael head of hosts,
Of Mary fair-skinned branch of grace,
Of Bride smooth-white of ringleted locks,
Of Columba of the graves and tombs,
   Columba of the graves and tombs.

Two Blessings: For Apples and First Fruits in Anglo-Saxon Tradition

These two blessings of apples and the 'new fruits' of the first harvest are taken from an eighth-century Anglo-Saxon liturgical book, the *Pontifical of St Egbert*, named after the archbishop of York who died in AD 766, an early collection of authentic and authoritative Anglo-Saxon texts.[66]

It is remarkable to see in the first prayer, the blessing of apples, a reference to Adam and Eve eating the forbidden fruit in the Garden of Eden, the patterns of biblical stories played out in the here and now of everyday life. This prayer also hints at the practice of holding an apple blessing on a particular saint's day during the harvest season, a prototype form of annual harvest festival which could easily be readopted today to focus on locally grown produce.[67]

1 Blessing of Apples

We pray to you almighty God that you bless this new fruit of apples, as you who forbade the eating of the deadly fruit of the apple tree to our forebears [Adam and Eve] with the just and utmost penalty of the sentence of death – paid through the manifestation of your one and only Son our Redeemer, our Lord and God Jesus Christ. And, through the benediction of the Holy Spirit, sanctify them all and bless them to be lifegiving, free and liberated from the ancient enemy and that first transgression of the insidious tempter. May we consume the diverse and edible fruits of the land during the solemnity of the anniversary of this day. Through Jesus Christ our Lord, who with the Father and Holy Spirit is worshipped and glorified, one God now and forever. **Amen.**

2 Blessing of New Fruits

Ruler of all ages, O Lord who provides all creatures at the opportune time, bless this your creature [the fruit or vegetables], and grant to bless us perpetually, and confidently raise up your power with the saints and your elect through Jesus Christ our Lord, who with the Father and Holy Spirit is worshipped and glorified, one God now and forever. **Amen.**

Harvest Blessing from the Apostolic Tradition

The Apostolic Tradition of Hippolytus is one of the oldest liturgical texts of the early Christian church, dating from the time of St Hippolytus of Rome in the early third century. It demonstrates in a number of ways how far the first Christians would orientate their prayer and ritual life around the natural world, not least in this charming short blessing prayer for the first fruits of the harvest. It has a curiously precise delineation of which plants and even flowers can and cannot be blessed, demonstrating a heightened awareness of their spiritual significance – and a pronounced antipathy towards garlic and other strong-smelling vegetables. The translation reproduced here is based on a translation from the Coptic text of the Apostolic Tradition.[68]

Blessing of the First Fruits

Only certain fruits may be blessed, namely grapes, the fig, the pomegranate, the olive, the pear, the apple, the mulberry, the peach, the cherry, the almond, the plum. Not the pumpkin, nor the melon, nor the cucumber, nor the onion nor garlic nor anything else having an odour. But sometimes flowers too are offered; here the rose and the lily may be offered, but no other. But for everything that is eaten shall they give thanks to the holy God, eating unto his glory.
As soon as first-fruits appear, all shall hasten to offer them to the bishop. And the bishop shall offer them, shall give thanks and shall name him or her who offered them, saying:

We give you thanks, O God, and we offer you the first fruits which you have given us to enjoy, nourishing them through your word, commanding the earth to bring forth fruits for the gladness and the food of men and all animals. For all these things we praise you, O God, and for all things with which you have blessed us, you who has adorned all creation for us with various fruits. Through your servant Jesus Christ, our Lord, through whom to you be glory, world without end.
Amen.

Blessing of Grapes and Beans

This short medieval prayer is directed at two seemingly distinct groups of agricultural produce, grapes and beans, perhaps because they are both grown on vines. It gives thanks for sunshine, rain and good weather, reflecting the concerns of the grower as well as the consumer of the produce. The blessing appears in the *Anderson Pontifical*, a book of liturgical material written in southern England sometime around the year AD 1000.

Blessing of Grapes and Beans

Lord bless this new fruit of grapes and beans which you, O Lord, deigned to lead to first maturity for our gathering by the warmth of the sun in the sky, inundation of rain and with bright and tranquil seasons by the action of your grace, in the name of our Lord Jesus Christ, who with the Father and Holy Spirit is worshipped and glorified, one God now and forever.
Amen.

A Prayer Against Lightning

This ritualized prayer is one of a number of nature-facing rituals recorded in the eighth-century liturgical book, the *Pontifical of St Egbert*, named after the archbishop of York who died in AD 766. The brief rubric is included below, indicating that holy water was sprinkled in the face of a storm, an arresting image and one that illuminates just how powerfully ritual action can be conceived as an agent for good in the natural world.[69]

Prayer Against Lightning

First blessed water is sprinkled and afterwards this prayer is said

Almighty and eternal God, have mercy on those who are anxious and show favour to our prayers that the power of the storm and the noxious fire of the clouds within it may pass over, by the promise of your power and glory through Jesus Christ our Lord, who with the Father and Holy Spirit is worshipped and glorified, one God now and forever.
Amen.

Order for the Blessing of Fields and Flocks: Roman Catholic Order

Gratitude for the blessings of God, for his creation and for entrusting it to the care of humans are all encapsulated in this rural service. It has been designed for any suitable occasion in an agricultural community, or as a way of marking the changes of the seasons and the changing patterns of farm labour.

This service is reproduced by kind permission of the International Commission on English in the Liturgy, and can also be found in the *Book of Blessings*.[70]

Blessing of Fields and Flocks

Minister: In the name of the Father, and of the Son, and of the Holy Spirit.

All make the sign of the cross and reply:

All: **Amen.**
Let us together praise the Lord, from whom we have rain from the heavens and abundance from the earth. Blessed be God now and for ever.
Amen.
Let us bless God, whose might has created the earth and whose providence has enriched it. He has given us the earth to cultivate, so that we may gather its fruits to sustain life.
But as we thank God for his bounteousness, let us learn

also, as the Gospel teaches, to seek first his kingship over us, his way of holiness. Then all our needs will be given us besides.

Reading

Reader: Brothers and sisters, listen to the words of the book of Genesis (Gen. 1.1, 11–12, 29–31a): God looked at everything he had made, and he found it very good. In the beginning when God created the heavens and the earth, God said, 'Let the earth put forth vegetation: plants yielding seed, and fruit trees of every kind on earth that bear fruit with the seed in it.' And it was so. The earth brought forth vegetation: plants yielding seed of every kind, and trees of every kind bearing fruit with the seed in it. And God saw that it was good. God also said, 'See, I have given you every plant yielding seed that is upon the face of all the earth, and every tree with seed in its fruit; you shall have them for food. And to every beast of the earth, and to every bird of the air, and to everything that creeps on the earth, everything that has the breath of life, I have given every green plant for food.' And it was so. God saw everything that he had made, and indeed, it was very good.

Psalm 65

The response to the psalm is: 'You answer us, O God our Saviour.'
You answer us, O God our Saviour.

You visit the earth and water it,
you greatly enrich it;
the river of God is full of water;
you provide the people with grain.
You answer us, O God our Saviour.

For so you have prepared the earth: you water its furrows abundantly, settling its ridges,
softening it with showers,
and blessing its growth.
You crown the year with your bounty;
your wagon tracks overflow with richness.
You answer us, O God our Saviour.

The pastures of the wilderness overflow,
the hills gird themselves with joy,
the meadows clothe themselves with flocks,
the valleys deck themselves with grain,
they shout and sing together for joy.
You answer us, O God our Saviour.

Intercessions

The Lord and Father of us all, looking with benign providence on his children, gives them nourishment and growth by blessing the earth with the fruitfulness that sustains human life. As children of this Father, let us pray to him, saying:
Lord, hear our prayer.

Assisting You have called us, as St Paul says, a field under your
Minister: cultivation; grant that by doing your will in all things we
may remain always close to you. For this we pray:
Lord, hear our prayer.

You have told us that Christ is the vine and we are the branches; grant that by living in your Son we may produce much good fruit. For this we pray:
Lord, hear our prayer.

You bless the earth and abundance flows in its pastures: grant that by your blessing our fields may yield the food we need. For this we pray:
Lord, hear our prayer.

You make the wheat grow that provides our daily bread and the gift of the Eucharist; give us a crop made rich by abundant rain and fertile soil. For this we pray:
Lord, hear our prayer.

You feed the birds of the air and clothe the lilies of the field; teach us not to worry about what we are to eat or drink or wear, but to seek first your kingship over us and your way of holiness. For this we pray:
Lord, hear our prayer.

Prayer of blessing

Minister: All-holy Lord and Father,
you have commanded us
to work the land and cultivate it.
Your devoted people now pray that you will grant us an
abundant harvest from our fields, vineyards and orchards.
In your goodness protect our lands from wind and hail
and let a rich crop grow
from the seeds we plant (today).
We ask this through Christ our Lord.
Amen.

May God, the source of every good,
bless us and give success to our work,
so that we may receive the joy of his gifts
and praise his name now and for ever.
Amen.

A concluding hymn can be sung

7

PILGRIMAGE PRAYERS
AND BLESSINGS

Nothing conjures up the notion of outdoor spirituality more than the call of the pilgrim path. An instinct for finding the divine beyond the confines of the church, temple and city walls can be traced right through Christian and Jewish history back to Exodus itself. For 40 years in the wilderness the Children of Israel followed God as a pillar of fire by night and a pillar of cloud by day. Less dramatic but no less spiritual are the many pilgrim routes available today, more popular now than they have been for centuries, since the days when medieval folk took to the road in search of healing and solace.

Pilgrimage is a free-ranging expression of spirituality, which is reflected in the diversity of rituals in this section. From private prayers and blessings suitable for the road all the way up to formal liturgical send-offs, there is something to suit every type of spiritual traveller. A few of the services involve the pilgrim's staff, an emblem of great power which is even used to draw a protective circle around the traveller in one early Anglo-Saxon rite.

As befits such an ancient tradition, the nature of pilgrimage has evolved over the centuries and continues to find new expression today. Originally a pilgrim was a wanderer, a traveller, a nomad or an exile, forsaking home but with no single holy destination in mind, not even a return journey back to the starting point. It was a state of detachment from the world, and even from the established church, and fairly quickly had its critics as a result. The Venerable Bede writing in the early eighth century reserved some harsh words for priests who 'love the wide journeyings of the world more than the enclosures of the Christian way of life'.

And so we present the following section of pilgrim blessings that reflect a rather more orderly, church-sanctioned attitude towards pilgrimage and travel more generally. The perils of the journey in earlier centuries may be of a different order and a different nature to those facing the open road today, but the spiritual significance remains undimmed. Indeed as a means of reconnecting with a truly cosmological sense of the sacred, there is little that compares with the fresh breeze and sense of hope at the start of any pilgrim path.

Anglo-Saxon Journey Blessings

These two journey blessings are taken from an eighth-century liturgical book, the *Pontifical of St Egbert*. A pontifical is a book of Christian rituals and the St Egbert in question is the archbishop of York who died in AD 766. This text has not previously been translated and presented in modern times and is revived here for pilgrims and all other travellers as a way of taking God's blessing into the landscape.

The first blessing has a threefold formula, seeking God's mercy, calling for the protection of angels, and praying for safe arrival – in both a spiritual and a literal sense. The traveller is compared to the Jewish people on their own journeys to the Promised Land, demonstrating the powerful way in which early medieval spirituality saw the whole landscape resounding with biblical and hence divine significance.

The second blessing contains even more powerful spiritual imagery, invoking the Archangel Raphael as a protector on the road. It makes references to the story of Tobias and his journey to Media in Persia to collect money owed to his father Tobit, from the deuterocanonical book of Tobit. It also refers to 'fires' both human and diabolical which a traveller might encounter, a concept we have translated as 'hazards'.[71]

1 For Those Going on a Journey

Minister: Almighty God, whose mercy is known in all places and who shows mercy through acts of service, direct their journey mercifully and lead them to the desired place unimpaired.

All: Amen.

May you merit the companionship of the perpetual company of angels now and also in all things to come; may you travel the rest of your journey unharmed with the consolation of their defence in departing and in returning.
Amen.

So may you make good the action and the way together, that you may both avoid the enticements of Egypt and come through via the way of justice to the prize of unfading joy.
Grant this Lord we beseech you, who with the Father and the Holy Spirit lives and reigns forever and ever.
Amen.

And the blessing of God Almighty, the Father, Son and Holy Spirit be with you now and for ever.
Amen.

2 *For Those Going on a Journey*

God, eternal giver of providence and lover of all, direct your way with the company of angels and by the prayers of the saints.
Amen.

May the great Raphael, guardian and guide of Tobias, be with you so that you may avoid hazards both human and diabolical, and be worthy to have the company of Christ, who is the way, the truth and the life.
Amen.

May his impregnable shield be yours in setting out and returning by which you may be saved from injury in mind and body, that you may obtain and keep whatever you desire with swift effect.
Grant this Lord we beseech you, who with the Father and the Holy Spirit lives and reigns forever and ever.
Amen.

And the blessing of God Almighty, the Father, Son and Holy Spirit be with you now and for ever.
Amen.

An Irish Blessing For Travellers

Wind, sun and rain all put in an appearance during this brief prayer of blessing for a journey, elements that are likely to be encountered for real on any pilgrim path in Britain and Ireland. Originally written in Gaelic and translated into English – or the other way round, depending on which authority you consult – the origins of this powerful blessing are a mystery but have been attributed to St Patrick himself, despite a lack of documentary evidence to support such a fine pedigree.

Irish Blessing

May the road rise up to meet you.
May the wind be always at your back.
May the sun shine warm upon your face;
the rains fall soft upon your fields and until we meet again,
may God hold you in the palm of his hand.

Prayer for Travelling

This short and poetic blessing for a traveller is included in the vast collection of oral traditions in the Highlands and Islands, gathered by the Scottish writer Alexander Carmichael.[72] It is replete with Christian imagery, as is so much of the material compiled across all six volumes of the *Carmina Gadelica*, reflecting the ancient and largely Catholic spirituality that Carmichael claimed to encounter on his journeys. While the origins of such oral material are difficult to verify, and there is evidence of a certain amount of editing work in producing the compilation, what is not in doubt are the very real landscapes conjured up, accompanied by a truly authentic sense of the sacred.

Prayer for Travelling

Life be in my speech.
Sense in what I say,
The bloom of cherries on my lips,
Till I come back again.

The love Christ Jesus gave
Be filling every heart for me.
The love Christ Jesus gave
Filling me for every one.

Traversing corries, traversing forests,
Traversing valleys long and wild.
The fair white Mary still uphold me,
The Shepherd Jesu be my shield,
The fair white Mary still uphold me.
The Shepherd Jesu be my shield.

Prayer to St James Prayed While Walking the *Camino*

This ancient prayer is said at the end of Masses at numerous stopping points along the Camino de Santiago, the 'Way of St James', a route which has been attracting pilgrims since at least the ninth century.[73] It is also widely presented as suitable for use on any other pilgrim journey, the greatest pilgrimage route in Europe offering a fine template for holy travellers everywhere. The final prayer at Santiago is certainly entirely appropriate for any pilgrim journey, calling as it does on St James, whose scallop symbol has become an emblem for pilgrims.

The Prayer

O God, who brought your servant Abraham out of the land of the Chaldeans, protecting him in his wanderings across the desert, we ask that you watch over us, your servants, as we walk in the love of your name to [*Santiago de Compostela/other destination*].
Be for us our companion on the walk,
Our guide at the crossroads,
Our breath in our weariness,
Our protection in danger,
Our lodging house on the *camino*,
Our shade in the heat,
Our light in the darkness,
Our consolation in our discouragements,
And our strength in our intentions.
So that with your guidance we may arrive safe and sound at the end of the road, and enriched with grace and virtue we return safely to our homes filled with joy.
In the name of Jesus Christ our Lord, Amen.
Apostle Santiago, pray for us.
Santa Maria, pray for us.
Amen.

The Blessing of Pilgrims:
Roman Catholic Order

The spiritual and pastoral value of pilgrimage is well remembered in this service, which has been designed for those about to set out on their journey. It places an emphasis on the traditional significance of the pilgrim experience, evoking the long traditions as well as the individual benefits to be had along the way and at the destination shrine or holy place.

This service is reproduced by kind permission of the International Commission on English in the Liturgy. Further blessing services, including a service for pilgrims on their return, can be found in the *Book of Blessings*.[74] The blessing of the pilgrims, which appears at the end of this service, could be used separately as part of another service such as Mass to mark the pilgrims' departure.

The Blessing of Pilgrims

Hymn or psalm

A suitable hymn or Psalm 122 is recommended to start the service

Celebrant: In the name of the Father, and of the Son, and of the Holy Spirit.

All make the sign of the cross and reply:

All: **Amen.**

May God, our strength and salvation, be with you all.
And with your spirit.

Brothers and sisters, as we set out, we should remind ourselves of the reasons for our resolve to go on this holy pilgrimage. The place we intend to visit is a monument to the devotion of the people of God. They have gone there in great numbers to be strengthened in the Christian way of life and to become more determined to devote themselves to the works of charity. We must also try to bring something to the faithful who live there: our example of faith, hope and love. In this way both they and we will be enriched by the help we give each other.

Reading

Reader: Brothers and sisters, listen to the words of the second letter of Paul to the Corinthians (2 Cor. 5.6–10): We are away from the Lord.
So we are always confident; even though we know that while we are at home in the body we are away from the Lord – for we walk by faith, not by sight. Yes, we do have confidence, and we would rather be away from the body and at home with the Lord. So whether we are at home or away, we make it our aim to please him. For all of us must appear before the judgement seat of Christ, so that each may receive recompense for what has been done in the body, whether good or evil.

Psalm 24

The response to the psalm is: LORD, this is the people that longs to see your face.
LORD, this is the people that longs to see your face.

The earth is the LORD's and all that is in it,
the world, and those who live in it;
for he has founded it on the seas,
and established it on the rivers.
LORD, this is the people that longs to see your face.

Who shall ascend the hill of the LORD?
And who shall stand in his holy place?
Those who have clean hands and pure hearts,
who do not lift up their souls to what is false,
LORD, this is the people that longs to see your face.

They will receive blessing from the LORD,
and vindication from the God of their salvation.

Such is the company of those who seek him,
who seek the face of the God of Jacob.
LORD, **this is the people that longs to see your face.**

Intercessions

Celebrant:	God is the beginning and the end of life's pilgrimage. Let us call on him with confidence, saying:
All:	**Lord, be the companion of our journey.**

Assisting
Minister:
Father all-holy, of old you made yourself the guide and
the way for your people as they wandered in the desert;
be our protection as we begin this journey, so that we
may return home again in safety. For this we pray:
Lord, be the companion of our journey.

You have given us your only Son to be our way to you;
make us follow him faithfully and unswervingly. For
this we pray:
Lord, be the companion of our journey.

You gave us Mary as the image and model for following
Christ; grant that through her example we may live a
new life. For this we pray:
Lord, be the companion of our journey.

You guide your pilgrim church on earth through the
Holy Spirit; may we seek you in all things and walk
always in the way of your commandments. For this we
pray:
Lord, be the companion of our journey.

You lead us along right and peaceful paths; grant that
we may one day see you face to face in heaven. For this
we pray:
Lord, be the companion of our journey.

Prayer of blessing

With hands outstretched, the celebrant continues with the prayer of blessing

All-powerful God,
you always show mercy towards those who love you
and you are never far away for those who seek you.
Remain with your servants on this holy pilgrimage

and guide their way in accord with your will.
shelter them with your protection by day,
give them the light of your grace by night,
and, as their companion on the journey,
bring them to their destination in safety.
We ask this through Christ our Lord.
Amen.

Concluding rite

Celebrant: May the Lord guide us and direct our journey in safety.
Amen.

May the Lord be our companion along the way.
Amen.

May the Lord grant that the journey we begin, relying
on him, will end happily through his protection.
Amen.

A concluding hymn can be sung

A Prayer Over Pilgrims from the *Sarum Missal*

A thousand years of tradition are brought to life by the recitation of the following ritual for pilgrims. Although written for church use, with an option that the service concludes with a Mass, the first section works particularly well as a pilgrim's blessing at the start of the road. Indeed the Mass itself does not take the shape of what would currently be celebrated in a church Eucharistic setting, although it could be used to augment a modern-day service, creating a truly traditional send-off.

The service comes from the venerable and distinctly English liturgical resource book known as the *Sarum Missal*, also known as the *Use of Sarum*. This was developed at Salisbury Cathedral from as early as the eleventh century, with material added right up to the Reformation. So distinctive are the traditions and rituals in this famous text, it is used by a wide range of churches even today, an authentic piece of early medieval spirituality which has a lasting influence on the Church of England.

The first section, which is recommended for use today, concludes with a blessing of the pilgrim's staff and 'scrip'. The original scrip was a leather purse or bag worn on a strap, best embodied today by a typical backpack or handbag.

Omitted from the text printed here is an additional section for pilgrims intending to walk to Jerusalem. Pilgrims then and now will no doubt be reassured to read that medieval canon law in the *Sarum Missal* expressly forbade one of the greatest trials that early travellers to the Holy Land had to endure, which was the practice of branding pilgrims with a cross on their flesh. The perils of producing a liturgical book promoting ancient rituals are as acute today as they were in medieval Salisbury. The Jerusalem section of the liturgy, along with the entire text of the *Sarum Missal*, can be found in English online, should anyone be considering a trip to Jerusalem.[75]

A Prayer Over Pilgrims

The following psalms are said over the pilgrims, or read alternately with pilgrims saying the even-numbered verses:

Psalm 91

Alternative psalms can be used here: the Sarum Missal suggests also Psalm 25 and Psalm 51.

Minister: You who live in the shelter of the Most High,
who abide in the shadow of the Almighty,

All: **will say to the Lord, 'My refuge and my fortress;**
my God, in whom I trust.'
For he will deliver you from the snare of the fowler
and from the deadly pestilence;
he will cover you with his pinions,
and under his wings you will find refuge;
his faithfulness is a shield and buckler.
You will not fear the terror of the night,
or the arrow that flies by day,
or the pestilence that stalks in darkness,
or the destruction that wastes at noonday.
A thousand may fall at your side,
ten thousand at your right hand,
but it will not come near you.
You will only look with your eyes
and see the punishment of the wicked.
Because you have made the Lord your refuge,
the Most High your dwelling place,
no evil shall befall you,
no scourge come near your tent.
For he will command his angels concerning you
to guard you in all your ways.
On their hands they will bear you up,
so that you will not dash your foot against a stone.
You will tread on the lion and the adder,
the young lion and the serpent you will trample under
foot.
Those who love me, I will deliver;
I will protect those who know my name.
When they call to me, I will answer them;
I will be with them in trouble,
I will rescue them and honour them.
With long life I will satisfy them,
and show them my salvation.

Glory to the Father and to the Son
and to the Holy Spirit;
as it was in the beginning is now
and shall be for ever. Amen.
Lord, have mercy upon us.

Christ, have mercy upon us.
Lord, have mercy upon us.
Our Father, who art in heaven,
hallowed be thy name;
thy kingdom come;
thy will be done on earth as it is in heaven.
Give us this day our daily bread;
and forgive us our trespasses as we forgive those who
trespass against us;
and lead us not into temptation,
but deliver us from evil.
I said, Lord, be merciful to me;
Heal my soul, for I have sinned against you.
The Lord show you his ways;
And teach us his paths.
The Lord direct your steps according to his word;
That no unrighteousness gets dominion over us.
O that your ways were made so direct;
That we might keep the statutes of the Lord.
The Lord uphold your goings in his paths;
That our footsteps slip not.
Blessed be the Lord God daily;
The God of our salvation prosper our way before us.
The good angel of the Lord accompany you;
And dispose our way and our actions aright, that we may
return again to our own place with joy.
Blessed are those that are undefiled in the way;
And walk in the law of the Lord.
Let the enemy have no advantage against you;
And let not the son of wickedness approach to hurt us.
O Lord, arise, help us,
And deliver us for your name's sake.
Turn us again, O Lord God of hosts;
And show the light of your countenance upon us, and we
shall be whole.
Lord, hear my prayer;
And let my cry come unto you.
The Lord be with you.
And with your spirit.

Collect

Let us pray.
Assist us, O Lord, in these our supplications, and dispose the way of your servants [*say names*] towards the attainment of your salvation, that among all the changes and chances of the journey through life, they may ever be defended by your help.
Through our Lord Jesus Christ, your son, who lives and reigns with you in the unity of the Holy Spirit, one God, for ever and ever. **Amen.**

Collect

Let us pray.
O God, who leads to life, and guards with your paternal protection those who trust in you, we beseech you that you would grant unto these your servants [*say names*] here present, going forth from among us, an escort of angels; that they, being protected by your aid, may be shaken by no fear of evil, nor be depressed by any lingering adversity, nor be troubled by any enemy lying in wait to assail them; but that having prosperously accomplished the course of their appointed journey, they may return to their own homes; and having been received back in safety, may pay due thanks to your name.
Through our Lord Jesus Christ, your son, who lives and reigns with you in the unity of the Holy Spirit, one God, forever and ever. **Amen.**

Collect

Let us pray.
O God, who ever bestows your pity on those who love you, and who are in no place far distant from those who serve you; direct the way of these your servants [*say names*] according to your will, that being their protector and guide, they may walk without stumbling in the paths of righteousness.
Through our Lord Jesus Christ, your son, who lives and reigns with you in the unity of the Holy Spirit, one God, for ever and ever. **Amen.**

The blessing of the staff and scrip

The pilgrims rise if previously sitting or kneeling, and the blessing of the scrip and staff follows:

The Lord be with you.
And with your spirit.

Let us pray.
O Lord Jesus Christ, who in your unspeakable mercy, and at the
bidding of the Father, and with the cooperation of the Holy Spirit,
did will to come down from heaven, and to seek the sheep that was
lost through the wiles of the devil, and to bear it back on your own
shoulders to the flock of the heavenly country, and commanded the
children of mother church by prayer to ask, by holy living to seek,
and by knocking to persevere, that they may be able to find more
quickly the rewards of saving life; we humbly beseech you that
you would vouchsafe to sanctify and bless + these scrips, and these
staffs, that whoever, for love of your name, shall desire to wear the
same, like the armour of humility, at their side, or to hang it from
their neck or shoulders, or to carry it in their hands, and so on their
pilgrimage to seek the prayers of the saints, with the accompaniment
of humble devotion, may be found worthy, through the protecting
defence of your right hand, to attain the joys of the everlasting vision,
through you, O Saviour of the world, who lives and reigns with the
Father and the Holy Spirit, ever one God, world without end.

*The priest sprinkles each scrip with holy water, and places it on the
pilgrim, saying to each one:*

In the name of our Lord Jesus Christ receive this scrip, the habit of
your pilgrimage; that after being well chastened you may be found
worthy both to reach in safety the thresholds of the saints where you
desire to go; and that when your journey is finished you may return
to us in safety.
Through our Lord Jesus Christ, your son, who lives and reigns with
you in the unity of the Holy Spirit, one God, for ever and ever.
Amen.

The priest hands a staff to each pilgrim, saying:

Receive this staff for the support of your journey, and for the labour
of your pilgrimage; that you may be able to overcome all the hosts
of the enemy, and to arrive in safety at the thresholds of the saints
where you desire to go; and that when your journey has been
obediently accomplished, you may again return to us with joy.
Through our Lord Jesus Christ, your son, who lives and reigns with
you in the unity of the Holy Spirit, one God, for ever and ever.
Amen.

An additional Mass for Travellers is included at the end of this liturgy in the Sarum Missal *text, and the following elements might be suitable for adding to a modern service:*

Be my strong rock, and house of defence: that you may save me. For you are my strong rock and my castle: be also my guide, and lead me for your name's sake.
(In Eastertide: Alleluia, alleluia)
In you, O Lord, have I put my trust; let me never be put to confusion, deliver me in your righteousness.

Collect

Assist us, O Lord, in these our supplications, and dispose the way of your servants [*say names*] towards the attainment of your salvation; that among all the changes and the chances of their journey through this life, they may ever be defended by your help.
Through our Lord Jesus Christ, your son, who lives and reigns with you in the unity of the Holy Spirit, one God, for ever and ever.

Reading

(Gen. 24.7)
The LORD, the God of heaven, who took me from my father's house and from the land of my birth, and who spoke to me and swore to me, 'To your offspring I will give this land,' he will send his angel before you.

Gradual

Be my strong rock and house of defence: that you may save me.
In you, O Lord, have I put my trust: let me never be put to confusion.
Be my strong rock and house of defence: that you may save me.
(In Eastertide: Alleluia.)

You that fear the Lord, put your trust in the Lord: he is their helper and defender.

Gospel

Reader: A reading from the Gospel according to Matthew 10.7–15. As you go, proclaim the good news, 'The kingdom of heaven has come near.' Cure the sick, raise the dead, cleanse the lepers, cast out demons. You received without

payment; give without payment. Take no gold, or silver, or copper in your belts, no bag for your journey, or two tunics, or sandals, or a staff; for labourers deserve their food. Whatever town or village you enter, find out who in it is worthy, and stay there until you leave. As you enter the house, greet it. If the house is worthy, let your peace come upon it; but if it is not worthy, let your peace return to you. If anyone will not welcome you or listen to your words, shake off the dust from your feet as you leave that house or town. Truly I tell you, it will be more tolerable for the land of Sodom and Gomorrah on the day of judgement than for that town.

Offertory

And all they that know your name will put their trust in you: for you, Lord, have never failed those who seek you. O praise the Lord who dwells in Sion. For he does not forget the complaint of the poor. **(In Eastertide: Alleluia.)**

Here the pilgrims make their offering; in the Sarum Missal *that clearly reflects a donation to the church but pilgrims might also like to offer up a prayer or hold an intention in their thoughts as they contemplate the journey ahead*

Prayer

Be favourable, we beseech you O Lord, to our supplications, and graciously receive these offerings which we present to you on behalf of your servants; that you would direct their way by your preceding grace, and accompany and follow them, so that we may rejoice in their safe performance of their journey by your merciful protection. Through our Lord Jesus Christ, your son, who lives and reigns with you in the unity of the Holy Spirit, one God, forever and ever.

If this service is followed by Communion, the following prayers are used

Prayer before Communion

You have charged that we shall diligently keep your commandments: O that my ways were made so direct that I might keep your statutes! **(In Eastertide: Alleluia, Alleluia.)**

Prayer after Communion

We beseech you, O Lord, that the reception of the sacrament of the heavenly mystery may further the good success of your servants' journey, and bring them to all things profitable to their salvation. Through our Lord Jesus Christ, your son, who lives and reigns with you in the unity of the Holy Spirit, one God, forever and ever.

After Communion, the minister shall say these following prayers over the pilgrims, whether they are travelling to Jerusalem, or to the threshold of St James, or on any other pilgrimage.

The Lord be with you.
And with your spirit.

Let us pray.
O God of infinite mercy and boundless majesty, whom neither space nor time separate from those whom you defend, be present with your servants [*say names*] who everywhere put their trust in you, and vouchsafe to be their leader and companion in every way in which they shall go: let no adversity harm them, no difficulty hinder them; let all things be healthful, and all things be prosperous for them; that whatsoever they shall rightly ask, they may speedily and effectually obtain by the aid of your right hand.
Through our Lord Jesus Christ, your son, who lives and reigns with you in the unity of the Holy Spirit, one God, forever and ever.

Collect

Let us pray.
May the almighty and everlasting God, who is the way, the truth, and the life, dispose your journey according to his good pleasure; may he send his angel Raphael to be your guardian in your pilgrimage; to conduct you on your way, in peace, to the place where you would go, and to bring you back again in safety on your return to us. May Mary, the blessed mother of God, intervene for you, together with all angels and archangels, and patriarchs, and prophets. May the holy apostles Peter and Paul intercede for you, together with the rest of the apostles, martyrs, confessors, and virgins; and may the saints whose prayers you ask, together with all the saints, obtain for you just desires, and prosperity, and remission of all sins, and life everlasting. Through our Lord Jesus Christ, your son, who lives and reigns with you in the unity of the Holy Spirit, one God, for ever and ever.

Then shall the pilgrims take Communion, and so depart in the name of the Lord

A Service for Pilgrims and Travellers

Where better to seek a pilgrim blessing than from the Irish church, founded by some of the greatest travellers in Christian history. Celtic explorers and adventurers include St Brendan, possibly the first European to visit the Americas, and St Patrick himself who made frequent journeys across the Irish Sea.

The following service is contained in a copy of *The Roman Missal* published in Cork in the last century, a compilation of standard liturgical material in the Roman Catholic Church that has some adaptations to local needs. This service is described as a Mass for pilgrims and travellers, although it does not include the Eucharistic liturgy as a Roman Catholic priest would need to officiate over a full service. Here it offers a meaningful collection of readings and prayers for those about to embark on an intentional journey.[76]

A Service for Pilgrims and Travellers

Opening psalm

Psalm 26

But as for me, I walk in my integrity; redeem me, and be gracious to me. My foot stands on level ground; in the great congregation I will bless the Lord.

Glory to the Father, and to the Son, and to the Holy Spirit: as it was in the beginning, is now, and will be for ever. Amen.

Collect

Hear, O Lord, our humble prayers, and set the course of your
servants in safety and prosperity, so that amid all the changes of life's
wayfaring they may ever be safeguarded by your help.
Through our Lord Jesus Christ, your son, who lives and reigns with
you and the Holy Spirit, one God, forever and ever.
Amen.

Reader: A reading from the book of Genesis 28.10–22.

Jacob left Beer-sheba and went towards Haran. He came
to a certain place and stayed there for the night, because
the sun had set. Taking one of the stones of the place, he
put it under his head and lay down in that place. And he
dreamed that there was a ladder set up on the earth, the
top of it reaching to heaven; and the angels of God were
ascending and descending on it. And the LORD stood
beside him and said, 'I am the LORD, the God of Abraham
your father and the God of Isaac; the land on which you
lie I will give to you and to your offspring; and your
offspring shall be like the dust of the earth, and you shall
spread abroad to the west and to the east and to the north
and to the south; and all the families of the earth shall be
blessed in you and in your offspring. Know that I am with
you and will keep you wherever you go, and will bring you
back to this land; for I will not leave you until I have done
what I have promised you.' Then Jacob woke from his
sleep and said, 'Surely the LORD is in this place – and I did
not know it!' And he was afraid, and said, 'How awesome
is this place! This is none other than the house of God, and
this is the gate of heaven.'

So Jacob rose early in the morning, and he took the stone
that he had put under his head and set it up for a pillar
and poured oil on the top of it. He called that place Bethel;
but the name of the city was Luz at the first. Then Jacob
made a vow, saying, 'If God will be with me, and will keep
me in this way that I go, and will give me bread to eat and
clothing to wear, so that I come again to my father's house
in peace, then the LORD shall be my God, and this stone,
which I have set up for a pillar, shall be God's house; and
of all that you give me I will surely give one-tenth to you.'

Gradual

Psalm 23 (not during Lent or Easter)

Even though I walk through the darkest valley, I fear no evil; for you are with me; your rod and your staff – they comfort me.
Alleluia, alleluia.

Psalm 119 (not during Lent or Easter)

Keep my steps steady according to your promise, and never let iniquity have dominion over me.
Alleluia.

The following seasonal psalms are said instead of the above during Lent and Easter

Psalm 91 (during Lent)

For he will command his angels concerning you to guard you in all your ways. On their hands they will bear you up, so that you will not dash your foot against a stone. You will tread on the lion and the adder, the young lion and the serpent you will trample under foot.

Psalm 119 and 122 (during the Easter season)

Alleluia, alleluia.
Keep my steps steady according to your promise, and never let iniquity have dominion over me.
Alleluia.
I was glad when they said to me 'Let us go to the house of the LORD!'
Alleluia.

Gospel reading

Reader: A reading from the Gospel according to Matthew 10.7–15. 'As you go, proclaim the good news, "The kingdom of heaven has come near." Cure the sick, raise the dead, cleanse the lepers, cast out demons. You received without payment; give without payment. Take no gold, or silver, or copper in your belts, no bag for your journey, or two tunics, or sandals, or a staff; for labourers deserve their food. Whatever town or village you enter, find out who in it is worthy, and stay there until you leave. As you enter the house, greet it. If the house is worthy, let your peace come upon it; but if it is not worthy, let your peace return to you. If anyone will not welcome you or listen to your words, shake off the dust from your feet as you leave that house or town. Truly I tell you, it will be more tolerable for the land of Sodom and Gomorrah on the day of judgement than for that town.'

Offertory

Psalm 17

My steps have held fast to your paths; my feet have not slipped. I call upon you, for you will answer me, O God, incline your ear to me, hear my words. Wondrously show your steadfast love, O saviour of those who seek refuge from their adversaries at your right hand.

The secret (said quietly)

Be appeased, O Lord, by our prayers and graciously accept these offerings which we make to you on behalf of your servants: send your grace before them to direct their steps, send it with them to accompany them, so that we may rejoice in their having, by your merciful help, accomplished their work and returned safely.
Through our Lord Jesus Christ, your son, who lives and reigns with you in the unity of the Holy Spirit, one God, for ever and ever.

If this service is followed by a Mass, the following two prayers are used

Communion prayer: Psalm 119

You have commanded your precepts to be kept diligently. O that my ways may be steadfast in keeping your statutes!

Post-communion prayer

May your sacraments, O Lord, which we have received, preserve your servants who hope in you; and defend them from all assaults of the enemy.
Through our Lord Jesus Christ, your son, who lives and reigns with you in the unity of the Holy Spirit, one God, forever and ever.

Anglo-Saxon or Celtic Journey Charm

This curious little devotional text is both prayer and charm, wishing good fortune on a traveller. It is densely packed with imprecations for protection provided by saint, prophets and Gospel writers, including a notable assembly of female saints, in addition to the biblical Eve. It appears in connection with the great Celtic leader St Cuthbert, perhaps a later addition to the traditions of his cult but invoking a powerful legacy of his rituals in the landscape.

The prayer starts with reference to 'fortification by a rod', and it is commonly assumed that this refers to the traveller drawing a circle around themselves on the ground with the base of the shaft of either a cross or more fittingly a pilgrim's staff. Drawing a circle is a ritualized symbol of protection from evil.

Mention of the charm's 'word-victory' and 'work-victory' probably refers to this ritual performance, the 'word' being the act of reciting the charm and the 'work' being the act of drawing the circle on the ground. A number of such charms are handed down from the early medieval period, referred to by the Anglo-Saxon word *galdor*, which clearly means a ritualized charm of considerable spiritual power. A *galdor* could be translated as an 'incantation', or perhaps more neutrally still a 'formula'.

This particular charm appears in just one Anglo-Saxon manuscript, as a note that a scribe has added to book four of the Venerable Bede's great *History* of the English church. In this section of the book, Bede is describing the famous seventh-century bishop of Lindisfarne St Cuthbert undertaking several important journeys, including his preparations before setting sail to Inner Farne Island. It seems possible that the scribe wanted to suggest that the saint performed this ritual before setting off on his travels. It also becomes clear that the 'journey' to be undertaken is considered both in terms of a literal journey and also the passage of a soul through life.

The text of this translation is slightly modernized from a nineteenth-century compilation of Anglo-Saxon charms and pieces of lore,[77] and the original Anglo-Saxon has been well analysed by a number of scholars.[78]

The Journey Charm

I encircle myself by this rod [*perhaps the shaft of a cross or base of a pilgrim staff*], and deliver myself into God's allegiance, against the sore sigh, against the sore blow, against the grim horror, against the great terror, which is loathsome to everyone, and against all the loathsome mischief which into the land may come: a triumphant charm I chant, a triumphant rod I bear, word-victory and work-victory: let this avail me, let no nightmare mar me, nor my belly trouble me, nor fear come on me ever for my life: but may the almighty heal me and his son and the comforter Spirit, Lord worthy of all glory, as I have heard, heaven's creator.

Abraham and Isaac and such men, Moses and Jacob, and David, and Joseph, and Eve, and Hannah and Elizabeth, Sarah and especially Mary, mother of Christ, and also a thousand of the angels I call to be a guard to me against all fiends. May they bear me up and keep me in peace and protect my life, uphold me altogether, ruling my conduct; may there be to me a hope of glory, hand over head [*a game easily won*], the hall of the hallows, the regions of the glorious and triumphant, of the truthful angels.

With cheerful mood I pray that for me, hand over head, Matthew be my helmet, Mark my coat of armour, my life's strong light, Luke my sword, sharp and sheer-edged, John my shield, embellished with glory. You Seraphim, guardians of the ways! Forth shall I depart, friends shall I meet, all the glory of angels, through the lore of the blessed one. Now I pray to the victor for God's mercy, for a good departure, for a good, mild, and light wind upon those shores; the winds I know, the encircling water, ever preserved against all enemies.

Friends I shall meet, that I may dwell on the almighty, yes, in his peace, protected against the loathsome one, who hunts me for my life, established in the glory of angels, and in the holy hand of the mighty one of heaven, while I may live upon earth.
Amen.

Prayer for One who Intends to Go on a Journey

This short formula of blessing for a journey is taken from a nineteenth-century Orthodox prayer book.[79] It takes an optimistic view of the benefits of travel, which by itself commends it as a positive way of setting off on any venture.

Orthodox Prayer for One Intending to Travel

God, our God, the true and living way, who did journey with your servant Joseph; journey with your servant [*name*] and deliver them from every storm and snare, and peace and vigour continually provide them. Be pleased that, having accomplished every intention of righteousness, according to your commandment, and being filled with temporal and heavenly blessings, they may return again.

For thine is the kingdom, and the power, and the glory, of the Father, and of the Son, and of the Holy Spirit, now and forever, and to the ages of ages.
Amen.

BIBLIOGRAPHY

Adamenko, Vasily Ivanovich, 1927, *Trebnik*, Nizhny Novgorod.

Adomnán, 1995, *Life of St Columba*, ed. Richard Sharpe, London: Penguin Classics.

Aitchison, N., 1994, *Armagh and the Royal Centres in Early Medieval Ireland*, Woodbridge: Cruithne Press.

Allen, Barbara, 2016, *Animals in Religion: Devotion, Symbol and Ritual*, London: Reaktion Books.

Arthur, Ciaran, 2018, *'Charms', Liturgies, and Secret Rites in Early Medieval England*, Woodbridge: Boydell Press.

Baring-Gould, S. and Fisher, J., 1911, *The Lives of the British Saints*, London: The Honourable Society of Cymmrodorion.

Bent, Helen, 2020, *Exploring Worship in Pilgrimage*, Cambridge: Grove Books.

Birch, Walter de Gray, ed., 1892, *Liber Vitae: Register and Martyrology of New Minster and Hyde Abbey, Winchester*, London: Simpkin & Co.

Blair, John, 2005, *The Church in Anglo-Saxon Society*, Oxford: Oxford University Press.

Bourne, Hugh, 1829, *A Collection of Hymns for Camp Meetings, Revivals etc. for the use of the Primitive Methodists*, Bemersley: Office of the Primitive Methodist Connexion.

Carmichael, Alexander, 1900, *Carmina Gadelica*, Vol. 1, Edinburgh: T & A Constable.

Celano, Thomas, 1908, *The Lives of St Francis of Assisi*, translated by A. G. Ferrers Howell, London: Methuen & Co.

Cennick, John, 1741, *Sacred Hymns for the Children of God, in the Days of their Pilgrimage*, London: B. Milles.

Chapman, David M., 2006, *Born in Song: Methodist Worship in Britain*, Warrington: Church in the Market Place Publications.

Church of England, 1890, *Certain Sermons or Homilies Appointed to be Read in Churches in the Time of Queen Elizabeth of Famous Memory*, London: SPCK.

Clough, David L., 2012, *On Animals: Systematic Theology*, London: T&T Clark.

Cockayne, Thomas Oswald, ed. and trans., 1864–66, *Leechdoms, Wortcunning, and Starcraft of Early England*. Rerum Britannicarum Medii Aevi Scriptores, Vol. 35. 3 vols, London: Longman.

Cooney, Jonathan, 'Creating Sacred Space Outdoors: The Primitive Methodist Camp Meeting in England, 1819–1840', *Thresholds* 25 (Fall 2002), pp. 43–7.

Cyril of Scythopolis, 1991, *The Lives of the Monks of Palestine*, trans. Richard Price, introduction by John Binns, Collegeville, MN: Liturgical Press.

Daneel, M. L., 1999, *African Earthkeepers, Vol. 2, Environmental Mission and Liberation in Christian Perspective*, Pretoria: UNISA Press

Easton, Burton Scott, 1934, *The Apostolic Tradition of Hippolytus*, Cambridge: Cambridge University Press.

Gittos, Helen and Sarah Hamilton, eds, 2016, *Understanding Medieval Liturgy*, Farnham: Ashgate Publishing.

Hapgood, Isabel Florence, trans., 1906, *Service Book of the Holy Orthodox-Catholic Apostolic (Greco-Russian) Church*, Boston, MA: Houghton, Mifflin & Co.

Hutton, Ronald, 1997, *Stations of the Sun*, Oxford: Oxford University Press.

International Commission on English in the Liturgy, 1989, *Book of Blessings*, New York: Catholic Book Publishing.

Jacob, Bishop of Edessa, 1901, *The Order of the Blessing of the Waters of the Epiphany*, trans. John, Marquess of Bute, London: Henry Frowde.

Jolly, Karen Louise, 2012, *The Community of St. Cuthbert in the Late Tenth Century: The Chester-le-Street Additions to Durham Cathedral Library A.IV.19*, Columbus, OH: The Ohio State University Press.

———, 1996, *Popular Religion in Late Saxon England: Elf Charms in Context*, Chapel Hill, NC: University of North Carolina Press.

Linzey, Andrew, 1999, *Animal Rites: Liturgies of Animal Care*, London: SCM Press.

Linzey, Andrew and Dan Cohn-Sherbok, 1997, *After Noah: Animals and the Liberation of Theology*, London: Mowbray.

Lott, David B. (ed.), 2007, *New Proclamation Commentary on Feasts, Holy Days, and Other Celebrations*, Minneapolis, MN: Fortress Press.

Mayhew-Smith, Nick, 2019, *The Naked Hermit*, London: SPCK.

McRae-McMahon, Dorothy, 2000, *Liturgies for the Journey of Life*, London: SPCK.

The Roman Catholic Church, 1938, *The Roman Missal*, Cork: Wm. Egan and Sons.

Rowe, Tamsin, 2010, *Blessings for Nature in the English Liturgy, c. 900–1200*, unpublished PhD thesis, University of Exeter.

Rupp, Katrin, 2008, 'The Anxiety of Writing: A Reading of the Old English Journey Charm', *Oral Tradition*, 23 (2), pp. 255–66.

Shann, G. V., trans., 1894, *Book of Needs of the Orthodox Church*, London: David Nutt.

Shanzer, D. and I. Wood, eds, 2002, *Avitus of Vienne: Letters and Selected Prose*, Translated Texts for Historians Vol. 38, Liverpool: Liverpool University Press.

Walsham, Alexandra, 2011, *The Reformation of the Landscape*, Oxford: Oxford University Press.

Warren, Frederick, trans., 1913, *The Sarum Missal in English, part 2*, London: A. R. Mowbray & Co.

Wesley, John, 1989, *The Works of John Wesley (Bicentennial Edition), Vol. 7: A Collection of Hymns for the Use of the People Called Methodists*, ed. Franz Hildebrandt and Oliver A. Beckerlegge, with James Dale, Nashville, TN: Abingdon.

Websites

www.letallcreationpraise.org.

www.methodist.org.uk.

www.umcdiscipleship.org/articles/the-love-feast.

www.katrinasdream.org.

fullhomelydivinity.org.

www.streetpastors.org.

www.missiontoseafarers.org.

http://sites.bu.edu/shonareligion/.

www.ealdfaeder.org/vo3/aecerbot.html.

www.archive.org.

ACKNOWLEDGEMENTS
OF SOURCES

Excerpts are taken from the English translation of *Book of Blessings* © 1987, International Commission on English in the Liturgy Corporation (ICEL): Blessing of Public Utilities; Blessing of a Bridge, Road and Other Means of Transport; Blessing of Sports Field or Gymnasium; Visiting a Cemetery; Blessing of Boats and Fishing Gear; Blessing of Seeds at Planting Time and The Blessing of Pilgrims. All rights reserved.

Excerpts are taken from *The small Missal*, 1938, London; Burns Oates & Washbourne.

The Roman Missal © 1938, Cork: Wm. Egan and Sons. A Hilltop Service for St Michael; A Service for Pilgrims and Travellers. All rights reserved.

Nick Utphall: Blessing of the Animals: A Short Service and Tree-planting Liturgy. Reproduced with his kind permission. Scripture quotations in Blessing of the Animals are taken from *THE MESSAGE*, copyright © 1993, 2002, 2018 by Eugene H. Peterson. Used by permission of NavPress. All rights reserved. Represented by Tyndale House Publishers, Inc.

Southwark Cathedral: Blessing of the River from a Bridge. Used by permission.

Ascension Trust: Prayers for Street Pastors. www.ascensiontrust.org.uk. Used by permission.

St Andrew's Church Wissett: Clipping Service. The text is reproduced by kind permission of the vicar and churchwardens.

Revd Barbara Allen: The Blessing of the Animals on St Francis' Day from her 2016 book, *Animals in Religion: Devotion, Symbol and Ritual*, London: Reaktion Books. Reproduced by permission.

Professor Karen Jolly: The Æcerbot Field Blessing, original text from Professor Jolly's 1996 publication, *Popular Religion in Late Saxon England: Elf Charms in Context*, Chapel Hill, NC: University of North Carolina Press, pp. 6–8. The text reproduced here by kind permission has been slightly updated by Professor Jolly for a forthcoming publication. Field Blessings from Anglo-

Saxon England, from Professor Jolly's 2012 publication, *The Community of St. Cuthbert in the Late Tenth Century: The Chester-le-Street Additions to Durham Cathedral Library A.IV.19*, Columbus, OH: The Ohio State University Press, pp. 212–13.

Professor Andrew Linzey's 'Celebrating the Creatures' and 'A Service for Animal Welfare' are taken from his *Animal Rites: Liturgies of Animal Care*, 1999, London: SCM Press. Both services are reproduced with kind permission from Wipf and Stock Publishers, www.wipfandstock.com.

Pan-Orthodox Concern for Animals: Prayer of St Tryphon. Reproduced here by kind permission. See panorthodoxconcernforanimals.org.

Pan-Orthodox Concern for Animals and Professor Andrew Linzey: Blessing for Animal Welfare Staff and Sanctuaries and Prayer at Death of Companion Animals composed by Fr Simon Peter Nellist, Archpriest of Tanzania, by combining traditional Orthodox intercessions and prayers with prayers composed by Professor Andrew Linzey. Produced here by kind permission. See panorthodoxconcernforanimals.org and www.oxfordanimalethics.com.

Dr Cynthia A. Wilson: Liturgy for a Love-Feast: A Time of Centring. Reproduced here by kind permission of Dr Wilson and available online at: www.umcdiscipleship.org/articles/the-love-feast.

Helene de Boissiere-Swanson: Liturgy for a Love-Feast: Katrina's Dream. Reproduced here by kind permission. For more information about Katrina's Dream see: www.katrinasdream.org.

Full Homely Divinity: Traditional Rogation Liturgy. Reproduced here by kind permission. For more information, see fullhomelydivinity.org.

Professor Marthinus L. Daneel: Tree-planting Eucharist from the 1996 publication *African Earthkeepers, Vol. 2, Environmental Mission and Liberation in Christian Perspective*, Pretoria: UNISA Press. Reproduced by permission.

FURTHER READING
AND RESOURCES

There are numerous modern books offering creative ways to conduct worship in and with the natural world, in addition to regularly updated resources through the websites of Britain's national churches. The Church of England has compiled a list of such resources, available here: www.churchofengland. org/resources/churchcare/advice-and-guidance-church-buildings/outdoor-wor ship. A range of resources connected to the Papal Encyclical *Laudato Si'* can be found here: cafod.org.uk/Pray/Laudato-Si-encyclical. And the Joint Public Issues Team, which brings together the Methodist Church, the Baptist Union, the Church of Scotland and the United Reformed Church, offers a compilation of its own material and helpful links: www.jointpublicissues.org.uk/issues/ environment.

Aisthorpe, Steve, 2020, *Rewilding the church*, Edinburgh: St Andrew Press.
Bent, Helen, 2020, *Exploring Worship in Pilgrimage*, Cambridge: Grove Books.
Gittos, Helen and Sarah Hamilton (eds.), 2016, *Understanding Medieval Liturgy*, Farnham: Ashgate Publishing.
Hargreaves, Sara, 2016, *Outdoor Worship: Engage with God in His Creation*, Bexleyheath: Music and Worship Foundation.
Heppenstall, Annie, 2015, *The Book of Uncommon Prayer*, Stowmarket: Kevin Mayhew.
Hollyhock, Juno, 2016, *Creative Ideas for Wild Church: Taking all-age worship and learning outdoors*, Norwich: Canterbury Press.
McRae-McMahon, Dorothy, 2000, *Liturgies for the Journey of Life* London: SPCK.
Papworth, Dan, 2016, *The Lives around Us: Daily Meditations for Nature Connection*, John Hunt Publishing.
Pratt, J. Wayne, 2013, *Worship in the Garden*, Nashville, TN: Abingdon Press.
Shakespeare, Steven, 2019, *The Earth Cries Glory: Daily Prayer with Creation*, Norwich: Canterbury Press.
Stanley, Bruce, 2013, *Forest Church*, Llangurig: Mystic Christ Press.
Summers, Rachel, 2017, *Wild Lent*, Stowmarket: Kevin Mayhew.
——, 2018, *Wild Advent*, Stowmarket: Kevin Mayhew.
——, 2019, *Wild Worship*, Stowmarket: Kevin Mayhew.

Ward, Tess, 2007, *The Celtic Wheel of the Year: Celtic and Christian Seasonal Prayers*, Ropley: O Books.

Welch, Sally, 2016, *Outdoor Church: 20 Sessions to Take Church Outside the Building for Children and Families*, Abingdon: Barnabas for Children.

Williams, Cate, 2019, *Forest Church: Earthed Perspectives on the Gospel*, Cambridge: Grove Books.

Woods, Rachel, 2016, *Into the Garden: Cultivation as a Tool for Spiritual Formation and Community Renewal*, Cambridge: Grove Books.

Woofenden, Anna and Sarah Miles, 2020, *This Is God's Table: Finding Church Beyond the Walls*, Harrisonburg, Virginia: Herald Press.

NOTES

1 Ronald Hutton, 1997, *Stations of the Sun*, Oxford: Oxford University Press.

2 Adomnán, 1995, *Life of St Columba*, ed. Richard Sharpe, London: Penguin Classics, iii.17, p. 219.

3 Jonathan Cooney, 'Creating Sacred Space Outdoors: The Primitive Methodist Camp Meeting in England, 1819–1840', *Thresholds* 25 (Fall 2002), pp. 43–7, at p. 44.

4 Alexandra Walsham, 2011, *The Reformation of the Landscape*, Oxford: Oxford University Press, p. 235.

5 Walsham, p. 241.

6 I investigated and recreated many such early hermit rituals for a previous study: Nick Mayhew-Smith, 2019, *The Naked Hermit*, London: SPCK.

7 S. Baring-Gould and J. Fisher, 1911, *The Lives of the British Saints*, London: The Honourable Society of Cymmrodorion, p. 67.

8 'Life of Sabas', chapter 27, in Cyril of Scythopolis, 1991, *The Lives of the Monks of Palestine*, trans. Richard Price, introduction by John Binns, Collegeville, MN: Liturgical Press, pp. 119–21.

9 N. Aitchison, 1994, *Armagh and the Royal Centres in Early Medieval Ireland*, Woodbridge: Cruithne Press, pp. 270, 277.

10 John Blair, 2005, *The Church in Anglo-Saxon Society*, Oxford: Oxford University Press, p. 475.

11 David L. Clough, 2012, *On Animals: Systematic Theology*, London: T&T Clark, pp. 149–51.

12 www.oxfordanimalethics.com.

13 Andrew Linzey, 1999, *Animal Rites: Liturgies of Animal Care*, London: SCM Press.

14 Vasily Ivanovich Adamenko, 1927, *Trebnik*, Nizhny Novgorod, pp. 227–9, translation by the author.

15 Barbara Allen, 2016, *Animals in Religion: Devotion, Symbol and Ritual*, London: Reaktion Books.

16 Alexander Carmichael, 1900, *Carmina Gadelica*, Vol. 1, Edinburgh: T & A Constable, p. 242.

17 Andrew Linzey, 1999, *Animal Rites: Liturgies of Animal Care*, London: SCM Press. Both services are reproduced with kind permission from Wipf and Stock Publishers, www.wipfandstock.com.

18 A quotation taken from Andrew Linzey and Dan Cohn-Sherbok, 1997, *After Noah: Animals and the Liberation of Theology*, London: Mowbray.

19 Thomas Celano, 1908, *The Lives of St Francis of Assisi*, translated by A. G. Ferrers Howell, London: Methuen & Co., pp. 296–8.

20 www.letallcreationpraise.org.

21 Scripture quotations in this liturgy are taken from *THE MESSAGE*, copyright © 1993, 2002, 2018 by Eugene H. Peterson. Used by permission of NavPress. All rights reserved. Represented by Tyndale House Publishers, Inc.

22 Hugh Bourne, 1829, *A Collection of Hymns for Camp Meetings, Revivals etc. for the use of the Primitive Methodists*, Bemersley: Office of the Primitive Methodist Connexion, preface.

23 It is also available from www.methodist.org.uk.

24 John Cennick, 1741, *Sacred Hymns for the Children of God, in the Days of their Pilgrimage*, London: B. Milles.

25 Available online at: www.umcdiscipleship.org/articles/the-love-feast.

26 *Methodist Worship Book* #119. Words: Delores Dufner, OSB Tune: Greensleeves.

27 *Methodist Worship Book* #2223.

28 For more information about Katrina's Dream see: www.katrinasdream.org.

29 David M. Chapman, 2006, *Born in Song: Methodist Worship in Britain*, Warrington: Church in the Market Place Publications, chapter 6, especially pp. 144–5.

30 John Wesley, 1989, *The Works of John Wesley (Bicentennial Edition), Vol. 7: A Collection of Hymns for the Use of the People Called Methodists*, ed. Franz Hildebrandt and Oliver A. Beckerlegge, with James Dale, Nashville, TN: Abingdon, pp. 695–700 for analysis of the hymn.

31 Avitus's *Homily 6* has been translated with introduction and notes by D. Shanzer and I. Wood, 2002, *Avitus of Vienne: Letters and Selected Prose*, Translated Texts for Historians Vol. 38, Liverpool: Liverpool University Press, pp. 381–8.

32 John Blair, 2005, *The Church in Anglo-Saxon Society*, Oxford: Oxford University Press, p. 473, for the earliest shapes of English Rogationtide processions.

33 Walter de Gray Birch, ed., 1892, *Liber Vitae: Register and Martyrology of New Minster and Hyde Abbey, Winchester*, London: Simpkin & Co. These two prayers are contained in a short section of the book focusing on blessing all kinds of produce, pp. 116–22. Translations by Revd Dr Sarah Brush.

34 International Commission on English in the Liturgy, 1989, *Book of Blessings*, New York: Catholic Book Publishing; this service is on pp. 391–9. The version reproduced here is suitable for use by a priest, deacon or lay minister.

35 fullhomelydivinity.org

36 Homilies and an exhortation for the days of Rogation week, in: Church of England, 1890, *Certain Sermons or Homilies Appointed to be Read in Churches in the Time of Queen Elizabeth of Famous Memory*, London: SPCK, pp. 502–33.

37 Alexandra Walsham, 2011, *The Reformation of the Landscape*, Oxford: Oxford University Press, p. 254.

38 International Commission on English in the Liturgy, *Book of Blessings*, 1989, New York: Catholic Book Publishing; this service is on pp. 371–81. The version reproduced here is suitable for use by a priest, deacon or lay minister. Alternative versions for priest and deacon only, and for a shorter blessing of an individual vehicle, are available in the book.

39 For more information about your local team, or to find out about establishing a new one, see www.streetpastors.org.

40 International Commission on English in the Liturgy, 1989, *Book of Blessings*, New York: Catholic Book Publishing; this service is on pp. 365–70, and is considered suitable for use by a priest or deacon.

41 International Commission on English in the Liturgy, 1989, *Book of Blessings*, New York: Catholic Book Publishing; this service is on pp. 733–40. The version reproduced here is suitable for use by a priest, deacon or lay minister.

42 Nick Mayhew-Smith, 2019, *The Naked Hermit*, London: SPCK.

43 Translation by Revd Dr Sarah Brush.

44 Translation by Revd Dr Sarah Brush.

45 The two books used as the basis for this text are: Isabel Florence Hapgood, trans., 1906, *Service Book of the Holy Orthodox-Catholic Apostolic (Greco-Russian) Church*, Boston, MA: Houghton, Mifflin & Co, pp. 189–97; G. V. Shann, trans., 1894, *Book of Needs of the Orthodox Church*, London: David Nutt, pp. 240–54.

46 Jacob, bishop of Edessa, 1901, *The Order of the Blessing of the Waters of the Epiphany*, trans. John, Marquess of Bute, London: Henry Frowde, pp. 79–101. The shorter blessing on the Eve of the Epiphany is on pp. 65–78.

47 www.missiontoseafarers.org.

48 Alexander Carmichael, 1900, *Carmina Gadelica* Vol. 1, Edinburgh: T & A Constable, pp. 213–15, 217.

49 St Brigid of Kildare.

50 International Commission on English in the Liturgy, *Book of Blessings*, 1989, New York: Catholic Book Publishing; this service is on pp. 388–9. The version reproduced here is suitable for use by a priest, deacon or lay minister.

51 www.letallcreationpraise.org.

52 M. L. Daneel, 1999, *African Earthkeepers, Vol. 2, Environmental Mission and Liberation in Christian Perspective*, Pretoria: UNISA Press, especially chapter 2, 'Green rituals and liturgies'. This book and much other related material, including fascinating further local theology about bad spirits and restitution, can be read online at: http://sites.bu.edu/shonareligion/introduction.

53 The verses quoted are recorded in nineteenth-century literature; for full citations see Ronald Hutton, 1997, *Stations of the Sun*, Oxford: Oxford University Press, pp. 46–7.

54 G. V. Shann, trans., 1894, *The Book of Needs of the Orthodox Church*, London: David Nutt, pp. 256–7.

55 Translation by Revd Dr Sarah Brush.

56 Adomnán, 1995, *Life of St Columba*, ed. R. Sharpe, London: Penguin Classics, book 2 chapter 44.

57 For a full discussion see John Blair, 2005, *The Church in Anglo-Saxon Society*, Oxford: Oxford University Press, p. 298.

58 The Roman Catholic Church, *The Roman Missal*, 1938, Cork: Wm. Egan and Sons, pp. 933–7.

59 Karen Louise Jolly, 2012, *The Community of St. Cuthbert in the Late Tenth Century: The Chester-le-Street Additions to Durham Cathedral Library A.IV.19*, Columbus, OH: The Ohio State University Press, pp. 212–13.

60 International Commission on English in the Liturgy, 1989, *Book of Blessings*, New York: Catholic Book Publishing; this service is on pp. 429–30. The version reproduced here is suitable for use by a priest, deacon or lay minister.

61 Karen Louise Jolly, 1996, *Popular Religion in Late Saxon England: Elf Charms in Context*, Chapel Hill, NC: University of North Carolina Press, pp. 6–8; the text reproduced here has been slightly updated by Professor Jolly for a forthcoming publication.

62 See www.ealdfaeder.org/vo3/aecerbot.html. Accessed on 26.12.2020.

63 Possibly meaning 'buckbean' or marsh trefoil, a bitter-tasting plant.

64 A *galdor* could be translated as an 'incantation', or perhaps more simply a 'formula'.

65 Alexander Carmichael, 1900, *Carmina Gadelica* Vol. 1, Edinburgh: T & A Constable, p. 165.

66 Translation by Revd Dr Sarah Brush, along with the similar blessing of grapes and beans on page 185.

67 Tamsin Rowe, 2010, *Blessings for Nature in the English Liturgy, c. 900–1200*, unpublished PhD thesis, University of Exeter, p. 183.

68 Burton Scott Easton, 1934, *The Apostolic Tradition of Hippolytus*, Cambridge: Cambridge University Press, p. 52.

69 Translation by Revd Dr Sarah Brush.

70 International Commission on English in the Liturgy, 1989, *Book of Blessings*, New York: Catholic Book Publishing; this service is on pp. 417–24, and is considered suitable for use by a priest, deacon or layperson.

71 Translation by Revd Dr Sarah Brush.

72 Alexander Carmichael, 1990, *Carmina Gadelica* Vol. 1, Edinburgh: T & A Constable, p. 321.

73 Among numerous quotations of this prayer, it is cited as part of the traditional Pilgrims' Mass in David B. Lott, ed., 2007, *New Proclamation Commentary on Feasts, Holy Days, and Other Celebrations*, Minneapolis, MN: Fortress Press, p. 153.

74 International Commission on English in the Liturgy, 1989, *Book of Blessings*, New York: Catholic Book Publishing; this service is on pp. 260–4, and is suitable for use by either a priest or deacon in Roman Catholic tradition.

75 Frederick Warren, trans., 1913, *The Sarum Missal in English, part 2*, London: A. R. Mowbray & Co, pp. 166–73; the omitted section for Jerusalem pilgrims is found on pp. 169–70. Text available online at www.archive.org.

76 The Roman Catholic Church, 1938, *The Roman Missal*, Cork: Wm. Egan and Sons, pp. 1370–4.

77 Thomas Oswald Cockayne, ed. and trans., 1864–66, *Leechdoms, Wortcunning, and Starcraft of Early England*. Rerum Britannicarum Medii Aevi Scriptores, vol. 35. 3 vols, London: Longman; Vol. 1, pp. 389–91.

78 The charm is discussed in some detail in Ciaran Arthur, 2018, *'Charms', Liturgies, and Secret Rites in Early Medieval England*, Woodbridge: Boydell Press, pp. 94–6; and also in Katrin Rupp, 2008, 'The Anxiety of Writing: A Reading of the Old English Journey Charm', *Oral Tradition*, 23 (2), pp. 255–66, at p. 263.

79 G. V. Shann, trans., 1894, *Book of Needs of the Orthodox Church*, London: David Nutt, 1894, p. 259.

LIST OF ILLUSTRATIONS

Pages

xv   Outdoor church service: www.istockphoto.com

xx   Rogation procession: www.newliturgicalmovement.org

1   Animal blessing: www.letallcreationpraise.org

3   Beehive blessing: https://cityroom.blogs.com/2012/06/19/the-blessing-of-the-bees

3   Bee on thistle: www.istockphoto.com

7   St Mammes of Caesarea: https://full-of-grace-and-truth.blogspot.com

9   St Francis: https://www.presentationparish.org

17   St Bride by John Duncan, 1913: https://www.commons.wikimedia.org

18   Pig farming: https://www.istockphoto.com

19   Animal blessing: https://www.commons.wikimedia.org

24   Working donkey: www.istockphoto.com

31   Guide dog: www.istockphoto.com

33   St Modestus: https://orthodoxwiki.org/Modestus_of_Jerusalem

35   Donkey sanctuary: https://www.donkeycarehome.co.uk

37   Pet grave: www.istockphoto.com

39   Outdoor gathering: www.istockphoto.com

42   Love feast: https://www.ncpedia.org/love-feasts

45   Revd Katrina Swanson: http://www.katrinasdream.org

47   Methodist love feast: https://www.commons.wikimedia.org

50   Rogation blessing: https://www.newliturgicalmovement.org

53   Clipping service: https://en.wikipedia.org/wiki/Clipping_the_church

57   Rogation blessing: https://www.newliturgicalmovement.org

63   Rogation Liturgy: https://www.newliturgicalmovement.org

79   Bishop John Buckley and Bishop Paul Colton perform a blessing ceremony at the reopening of St Patrick's Bridge, Cork: https://churchofirelandcork.com

83   Street pastor: https://www.ascensiontrust.org.uk/street-pastors

90   Cemetery blessing: https://stmatthewskenton.org

95   Well dressing at Tissington, Derbyshire: https://en.wikipedia.org/wiki

98   Anglo-Saxon water blessing: https://anglosaxonwater.wordpress.com

101   Great blessing of the waters: https://www.commons.wikimedia.org

114   Delegation from Southwark Cathedral annual blessing of the Thames: https://calendarcustoms.com

128   Blessing of boats: https://www.theday.com

140   Coastal life: https://en.wikipedia.org/wiki

145   Detail of Jesse Tree window at St Mary's, Shrewsbury, 14th century: https://en.wikipedia.org/wiki

147   Tree planting liturgy: https://msjroscrea.ie

151   Image of Tree of Life with Christ and the Twelve Apostles, Greek orthodox, 15th century: https://www.commons.wikimedia.org

161   Fields, hills, weather and agriculture: https://www.istockphoto.com

164   St Michael, Fra Filippo Lippi, 1456: https://www.commons.wikimedia.org

169   Agricultural revolution in Anglo-Saxon England: https://www.archaeology.wiki/blog

172   St Tryphon, www.johnsanidopoulos.com

179   Blessing of first grain and blessing a bakery: https://www.istockphoto.com

181   Reaping: https://www.oldbookillustrations.com

187   Blessing of fields: https://www.istockphoto.com

192   Anglo-Saxon pilgrims: https://intriguing-history.com

196   Sign on the Camino de Santiago: https://www.istockphoto.com

197   The Latin Mass Society pilgrimage to Walsingham: https://www.walsingham.org.uk

209   Statue of St Patrick at the beginning of the pilgrimage route to the summit of Croagh Patrick: www.carrowkeel.com